MY SON,
GIVE ME YOUR HEART

A devotional book for young men
to live Christ-centered lives
for the glory of God

Sonny L. Hernandez

Reforming America Ministries
Clarksville, TN
www.ReformingAmericaMinistries.com

Unless otherwise indicated, Scripture quotations are from The Holy Bible, New
King James Version (NKJV), copyright © 2001 by Crossway Bibles, a division
of Good News Publishers. Used by permission.
Cover design by Sonny Jr.

My son, give me your heart,
And let your eyes observe my ways
(Prov. 23:26).

DEDICATION

For Sonny Jr.

I will never forget our *father and son* Bible study times at the local coffee shop we used to visit, or the times we spent singing hymns, reciting the Nicene Creed, praying, weeping, and reading Scripture together during our family worship—which I always called the best part of the day—and the most precious times of my life.

My son, please forgive me for the times I failed to lead you in a biblical manner. I pray that you will believe in the gospel, love God's Word, weep over your sin, and live your life to the glory of God.

The righteousness of Christ is the only grounds of justification, and assurance of salvation.

I love you.

CONTENTS

AUTHOR'S PREFACE

My son, if you receive my words,
And treasure my commands within you,
So that you incline your ear to wisdom,
And apply your heart to understanding;
Yes, if you cry out for discernment,
And lift up your voice for understanding,
If you seek her as silver,
And search for her as for hidden treasures;
Then you will understand the fear of the LORD,
And find the knowledge of God
(Prov. 2:1-5).

My Son, Give Me Your Heart is a devotional book that was written for young men. God's Word is the only protection young men have against the wicked things in this world. This book was also written for fathers, which could strengthen their relationships with their sons. Thus, fathers should read this book with their sons as a Bible study guide that honors and glorifies Christ.

This devotional book could prevent young men from receiving misconduct allegations and stumbling into wicked patterns. This is important. Allegations can lead to arrests, jail, or prison, while accepting a false gospel can lead to offending God, death, and then the judgment. Young men need to be shown how to avoid being put into the position of receiving an allegation. This book will show young men how to think biblically before they do something dishonoring to the Lord.

There are some young men who listen to sound wisdom, while others are forced to learn the hard way, so to speak. Young men can either learn from others in this life and in Scripture (who suffered temporally and eternally for their unwise choices), or they will be the ones who show others how to be wise (because they suffered for making unwise decisions). This is why God's Word commands fathers to raise their children in the admonition and fear of the Lord.

This book focuses on biblical wisdom, not legalism.[1] *Legalism* is the belief that one must perform an act or meet a certain condition to be saved or in order to know if one is saved or not. This belief [legalism] must be rejected as heresy. One's obedience, good works and law-keeping are not the grounds of salvation or assurance of salvation.

Salvation is by grace alone (source of justification), through faith alone (instrument of justification), in Christ alone (grounds of justification), according to Scripture alone, to the glory of God alone. Therefore, this book does not advocate legalism; it advocates for teaching biblical truths and gospel principles that are found in Scripture.

Young men must be taught how to be wise. Watching movies, texting on cell phones, playing video games, hanging out at social events, and being involved in sports will never make them wise in salvation. Instructing them with godly wisdom will. This is why fathers must teach their sons about the fear of the Lord, and the gospel of Jesus Christ, or false teachers will instruct them to despise God's Word and everything in it.

Sonny L. Hernandez

---

[1] **Important disclaimer**: This book will teach about *many* biblical truths, which are not conditions of salvation. The righteousness of Christ is the only grounds of justification, and assurance of salvation. Therefore, when reading this book, do not be misled into thinking that *many* of the biblical truths in this book (important, and must be taught) are conditions or assurance of salvation. For example, the Bible teaches that believers are to be baptized in the name of the Triune God. This is called the *Great Commission*, which must be taught. However, baptism is a command and it is important, but it does not save.

IMPORTANT MESSAGE FOR FATHERS

Children are young plants which must be watered with good education, so that they may, with Obadiah, fear the Lord 'from their youth up' (I Kings 18:12). Plato said, 'In vain does he expect a harvest who has been negligent in sowing.' Nor can a parent expect to reap any good from a child, where he has not sown the seed of wholesome instruction. And though, notwithstanding all counsel and admonition, the child should die in sin, yet is it a comfort to a godly parent to think that before his child died, he gave it a spiritual medicine.

—Thomas Watson

TO FATHERS: You must never forget that your child is a "heritage from the LORD" (Ps. 127:3), and that you have a responsibility to train up your child in the way that he should go, so when he is old, he will not depart from it (Prov. 22:6). With fervent prayer, godly discipline, and the Holy Spirit's guidance, you will emulate the words from the apostle John who said: "I have no greater joy than to hear that my children walk in truth" (3 John 4).[2]

Raising children will come with many difficulties. For one, they are sinners, and two, so are you. Therefore, your child will struggle with sin, and so will you. This book will show you how to be wise. Living in a sinful world, and being sinful creatures, you must disciple and equip your son to serve God and to protect himself from the evil one. Most importantly, you must be wise, and teach your son the true gospel.

---

[2] Prayer and godly discipline cannot earn favor with God, nor are they conditions of salvation. Prayer and godly discipline are important biblical truths, which must be taught. Put another way, according to the Bible, parents must pray for their children, and exercise discipline. However, parents must never think that their prayers or teachings on godly discipline are conditions or assurance of salvation.

Please allow me the opportunity to confess something very important to you. As a preacher, I will never forget the time I was a pastor of a Reformed Baptist church plant. During this time, I was constantly busy. I dedicated innumerable hours to ministry, but (shamefully) I failed to lead the most important ministry that God had given to me: My family. That is right. I wasted precious opportunities to shepherd my wife and son—which is a time I will never get back.

Neglecting precious time to shepherd my wife and son was one of the worst offenses I have ever committed in my life. Consequently, my son stumbled into sinful patterns in school that caused the principal to arrange a time for me to meet with her husband—the headmaster of the school—who was also a seasoned pastor. During this visit, the headmaster was very kind, and he treated me the way a father would treat his son. I will never forget what he said to me. He said [paraphrased]:

> "Sonny, I know you and I don't know each other very well, but I am convinced that you are spending a lot of time shepherding your congregation, which is honoring, but you are neglecting your son, which is horrible. This is not practicing what you preach. As a preacher, you cannot manage the church of God, if you cannot manage your home. Your son needs his father to shepherd him daily, and to discipline his sinful patterns. This is the love that he needs right now, but will not receive it if you spend so much time caring for others, while simultaneously neglecting your family at home."

After hearing this pastor's message, I remained silent, and felt broken spiritually. I realized that he was absolutely correct. I thanked the pastor for speaking to my heart, then I went home, and wept uncontrollably to my wife over my guilt. And for good reasons. First Timothy 5:8 reads: "**But if anyone does not provide for his own, and especially for those of his household, he has**

denied the faith and is worse than an unbeliever" (emphasis mine). I repented to God for neglecting my family, and I also repented to my son.[3] That's right. I confessed my sins to my son, and I wept to him. I begged for his forgiveness. This is what I pray you will do as well.

You must confess your sins to your son. As a Christian, it is easy to make mistakes raising a child—who have not been born again. There are times that you will blame your child for something he did wrong without realizing that you may be at fault as well. Consider this illustration:

> Two businessmen decided to travel overseas to finalize a contract with a large manufacturing company. Therefore, these two businessmen decided to hire a general manager to lead their large organization in the United States, which had hundreds of employees, and thousands of customers. After a long travel, the two business owners returned to find their once successful business with pending lawsuits, several customer complaints, and their reputation tarnished. Who are the two business owners going to confront upon their return? It is going to be the general manager. The general manager was the one *left in charge* of the production.

Therefore, who is God going to hold accountable for a house that is not managed biblically? It is going to be the father—the head of his household—who was left in charge by God to lead his wife and son.

As a sinner, you should make it a habit to confess your sins to your son, especially since sin is a practice that you will commit on a daily basis. Remember, your son will follow your steps, on many

---

[3] Repentance does not precede regeneration, nor does it merit God's favor. Repentance is a gift of God—which is given to the elect—after they have been born again.

occasions. This is why you want your son to follow biblical steps. If you do not make it a practice to confess your sins to your son—when your child falls into sin—you may put the blame on him. This means that your child will be raised by a father who taught him that being a man requires one to blame others, and not accept responsibility. A father, one who fears God and loves his son, will follow James' counsel: "Confess your trespasses to one another, and pray for one another, that you may be healed…" (5:16).

Follow one of the examples of Jacob Marley, a fictional character in the classic book, *A Christmas Carol*. In this novella, Marley appeared to Ebenezer in chains, warning him to avoid making the same mistakes that he had made in life, or else Ebenezer would end up just like he did in death: Bound to chains, and sealed in darkness. This is an excellent illustration.

Teach your child to never follow your past mistakes, or that of others, or else he will end up suffering the consequences because he refused to listen. Children who are unregenerate need Christ declared to them, and they need to be warned about the dangers of not obeying the gospel of our Lord Jesus Christ (2 Thess. 1:8).

Raising a child can be difficult, but you must not place unreasonable expectations on him. It would do a doctor no good to treat a dying cancer patient like he would a marathon runner who was showing up for a routine physical. This does not mean that you should neglect your responsibility to lead your child (biblically), nor does it mean that you should allow worldliness to creep into your home. Absolutely not!

Raising a child that may not be saved requires you to be the example to him. Therefore, Christians parents should do the following:

- Preach the gospel to your child (daily).
- Be patient when your child does wrong.
- Stay loving when your child sins and upsets you.
- Discipline your son's wrongdoing, without lambasting him.
- Do not provoke your son to anger.
- Teach your child to hate the things that God hates and to love the things that God loves.
- Pray that God will extract your son's stony heart of flesh, and implant a new heart into him that will beat for Christ.

Additionally, I will explain several reasons why you should not affirm your child's Christianity if he does not have a credible profession of faith.

First, it will mislead your child to believe he is regenerate. As a result, he may go through life with a false sense of eternal security, and may rely on works to justify his delusion. Therefore, make sure that your son knows and believes the true gospel before you affirm his profession of faith.

Second, your child will not get the spiritual care he needs if you are misleading him to believe he is already a Christian. Doctors provide loving care to dying patients by telling them that they are dying. Doctors also provide the patient with the cure so they can heal. Therefore, you must treat your child with the same care, and pray. If your son is not converted, preach the gospel. The true gospel is mighty to save.

Third, you may place unrealistic expectations on your child, and it may provoke him to anger. You must be careful with this, and remember that your child is only a child. If your child is unregenerate, you cannot expect him to like or follow what regenerate people like. Unconverted children do not have the desire to love godly things. You must be patient, and pray that God will give your son a new heart to love the things that God loves. This will help you to avoid provoking your child to anger.

Do you truly desire to raise your child (biblically) in the nurture and admonition of the Lord? If you do, it is imperative that you do not provoke your son to anger. There are several ways that fathers provoke their children to anger:

- They will make screaming a habit every time their child does something wrong.
- They will not be consistent in disciplining their child.
- They will say disparaging things to their children to motivate them or they will compare them to others.
- They will rarely say uplifting comments to their children when they do things correctly.
- They will not be the example to their child on how to live in fear of God.

All of these things are examples that will provoke your son to anger. Nothing good comes from anger! Young men are capable of committing irrational and irreconcilable acts when they are provoked to anger. You need to follow the advice from Paul. The apostle said, **"And you, fathers, do not provoke your children to wrath, but bring them up in the training and admonition of the Lord"** (Eph. 6:4; emphasis mine).

How can you avoid provoking your son to anger? When your child does something wrong, remind your child that his sin is ultimately not against you; it is against the Lord. Do not ever scream at your child! Correct your child with patience and love, reminding your son that you do not hate him, but love him and want him to be restored, not ostracized.

Do not forget to discipline your child. If you do not discipline your child, you are sending the following message to him: he is not valued by you, you don't care that he could suffer worse consequences in the future, and the Bible does not matter to you since God's Word commands you to discipline your child in love (Prov. 13:24; 23:13-15).

When you discipline your child, do not ever say disparaging things to your child, or compare him to others. Your goal is to reform your child, not reject him, and your goal in parenting is to compare them with the Bible, not with their buddies. In your discipline, make sure that you are commending your child more than you are correcting them. Otherwise, your child may find himself more discouraged than disciplined. Again, remember Paul's guidance: "Fathers, do not provoke your children, lest they become discouraged" (Col. 3:21).

Be the example your son can follow. If you love your son, read the Bible to him daily, preach the gospel to him daily, pray with him or for him daily, weep for his soul daily, and be the Christian example he can follow daily. Raise your child to love Christ, teach him to despise worldly things, and confess your sins to your son when you are wrong. Lord willing, when he grows old, he will not depart from the faith. Either you teach your son about the Savior's righteousness, or the world will teach him self-righteousness.

Worldly parents do not and will not follow these aforementioned examples. Instead, they will do the following:

- They will buy their young children cell phones, which means they will have direct access to look at every worldly thing they desire (1 John 2:15-17).

- They will let them hang out with their worldly friends despite the fact Scripture warns that "bad company ruins good morals" (1 Cor. 15:33).
- They will allow them to watch movies that have innumerable coarse words and blasphemous rhetoric that God hates (Exod. 20:7; Prov. 8:13).
- They will show excitement about sports, hobbies, social events, and vacations, but will not show excitement about their local church or sharing the gospel to their children.

Parents who follow these examples are not declaring the Savior to their children; on the contrary, they are delivering them over to Satan. Once their children grow up, they will run off into the world like a caged animal runs away from its captors when they are set free.

When worldly children grow up and are on their own, they will lavish the world, and not the Word. They will only think about temporal happiness, not eternal holiness. Additionally, when they are in need of help, worldly children will not seek a pastor who will teach them about the dangers of sin and the gospel of Christ. Worldly children will run to psychologists who will drug their minds and empower them to be self-centered victims. This is what happens when children follow worldly examples: Their parents.

If you allow these things to happen, wake up! Your child is a gift from God. If God gave you a child, what kind of child is he going to be when he grows up and you send him off into the world? Either you are going to faithfully raise your son in the admonition and discipline of the Lord, or you will live your life making excuses for why you neglected the precious life of your child whom God gave to you as a gift. Again, wake up, before it is too late!

Another way you can be the example to your son is by showing him how to love his future wife. You must be the example to him. Never forget that the way a man treats his wife is a direct reflection of how he loves Christ. Your children will see this.

Marriage is not easy. At times, marriage can be very difficult. But you must never forget that marriage between a man and a woman is a reflection of the marriage between Christ and His bride—the church. Teach your son how to love his future wife by loving your wife, even when she is ornery and sinful. Therefore, show compassion, patience, and love to your wife. Your son is watching.

One of the most important disciplines in your life that you must practice is daily worship. This is non-negotiable. Leading your home in family worship is the most critical part of your child's life. In my opinion, family worship will be the most memorable times that your child will remember when he is all grown up. When you lead your family in worship, preach the gospel of Christ, sing hymns, and read the Bible together. This should be completed *daily*.

Additionally, make it your prerogative to disciple your son every day. You need your son's undivided attention as you diligently and prayerfully instruct him. Therefore, find a coffee shop, restaurant, or a quiet place in your home so you can teach your son how to be wise. There are roughly thirty-one days in a month. Therefore, you will not go wrong by teaching your son the Proverbs every day, especially since it has thirty-one chapters that are full of wisdom for young men. Most importantly, you must declare the gospel to your son. This will serve as a perfect opportunity for you to strengthen your relationship with your son.

Read John Bunyan's sermon *"The Christian Family."* He will share some insight on how to manage your son biblically if he becomes rebellious. If you have a son who will not listen to your biblical teachings, and will not attend church, do not permit him to disobey you or not attend church. You are commanded by God to manage your son, not allow your son to manage you.

If your son is disobedient to your leadership, follow the previous guidance that I shared with you, and pray that God would reveal the following to you:

- Why have you failed to manage your household biblically?
- Why does your son disrespect you?

Pray that God will discipline you to lead your home biblically. Next, invite men from the church and other pastors into your home to preach and plead to your son's soul. If you do not invite other pastors and men from the church, you will be forced to rely on psychologists and medicine to lead and discipline your son since you could not. God forbid!

In closing, parenting, as you can see, will require a PhD. This acronym stands for prayer, the Holy Spirit, and discipline. If you love your son, you must tell him, "My son, give me your heart." That is, my son, give me your undivided attention. Lord willing, your son may thank you for it when he is old, and has not departed from it.

CHAPTER I.
MY SON, FEAR THE LORD &
DEPART FROM EVIL

Christian, let God's distinguishing love to you be a motive to you to fear Him greatly. He has put His fear in your heart, and may not have given that blessing to your neighbor, perhaps not to your husband, your wife, your child, or your parent. Oh, what an obligation should this thought lay upon your heart to greatly fear the Lord! Remember also that this fear of the Lord is His treasure, a choice jewel, given only to favorites, and to those who are greatly beloved.

—John Bunyan

My son, every day you rise up from your sleep, do not be naïve that life is perfect and nothing perilous exists. On the contrary, life is a spiritual warzone! If you turn on the news, you will see just how bad the war truly is. The spiritual battlefield is far worse than any war the United States has ever engaged in. You are part of this war. As a sinner, you will be tempted to do wicked things. You will have wicked thoughts, and will act out on many of them. The sin you commit is dishonorable to your parents, but it's also a crime to God.

The war between good and evil has existed for a long time. In the beginning of creation, the serpent, who was a manifestation of the devil, temped Adam and Eve to transgress the law of God (Gen. 3:1-5). This is why terrible things happen in this life: Sin entered into the human race. If you study the Bible, you will see that Adam and Eve are not the only ones Satan has harmed. Throughout history, the devil has roamed the earth (Job 1:6-12), he accused Joshua (Zech. 3:1-2), he tempted the incarnate Christ (Matt. 4:1-11), he caused Ananias to lie to the Holy Spirit (Acts 5:3), and his messenger tormented the apostle Paul (2 Cor. 12:7). Satan does not care about your race, religion, national origin, etc.

Satan is an equal opportunity deceiver. Therefore, do not ever think that he will not tempt or try to deceive you. If you try to contend with him (without God), you will certainly fail and perish. Carefully examine Jude 9 to see how the archangel Michael responded:

> Yet, Michael the archangel, in contending with the devil, when he disputed about the body of Moses, dared not bring against him a reviling accusation, but said, "The Lord rebuke you!"

You need to be aware of how Satan will try to trap you. For the devil, catching a child in sin is really no different than catching a mouse. To catch a mouse, all you would need to do is hide a sticky mousetrap in an inconspicuous area and place a small piece of cheese in the center. It would be impossible for the mouse to eat the cheese unless it takes the first step, where it will be subdued by the sticky trap. In the same manner, all the devil has to do is set up a trap that will afford you with the opportunity to act upon your sinful desires. The devil will place the cheese—which are things that will tempt you—in the center of his trap. You must not fall for these devices!

When you sin, it is not so much that you have sinned against your neighbor or your friend. Sinning is an offense to God. Therefore, when you sin in what you think is a private place where no one is looking, you need to think again. According to Proverbs 15:3, "The eyes of the LORD are in every place, keeping watch on the evil and the good." Job 34:21 also states, "For His eyes are on the ways of man, and He sees all his steps." Know these verses well, my son. For example, if a young man is struggling with masturbation or porn, and he thinks that he can find a discreet place where he can act out on his sinful desires, he needs to be reminded that his carnal actions are never discreet before God. The

Lord sees and knows all things. Pay careful attention to David's words in Psalm 139:1-6:

> O LORD, You have searched me and known me.
> **You know my sitting down and my rising up;**
> **You understand my thought afar off.**
> **You comprehend my path and my lying down,**
> **And are acquainted with all my ways.**
> **For there is not a word on my tongue,**
> **But behold, O LORD, You know it altogether.**
> You have hedged me behind and before,
> And laid Your hand upon me.
> Such knowledge is too wonderful for me;
> It is high, I cannot attain it (emphasis mine).

In his book *Thoughts for Young Men*, J.C. Ryle provided an excellent testimony on the dangers of thinking that God cannot see our sins in secret:

> Endeavor, I beseech you all, to realize this fact. Recollect that you have to do with an all-seeing God—a God who never slumbereth nor sleepeth (Psa. 121:4)—a God who understands your thoughts afar off, and with whom the night shines as the day (Psa. 139:2, 12). You may leave your father's roof, and go away, like the prodigal into a far country (Luke 15:13), and think that there is nobody to watch your conduct; but the eye and ear of God are there before you. You may deceive your parents or employers, you may tell them falsehoods and be one thing before their faces, and another behind their backs, but you cannot deceive God. He knows you through and through. He heard what you said as you came here today. He knows what you are thinking of at this minute. He has set your most secret sins in the light of his countenance, and they will one day come out before the world to your shame, except you take heed (1 Cor. 4:5).[4]

---

[4] J.C. Ryle, *Thoughts for Young Men*. (Carlisle, PA: Banner of Truth, 2015), 61. Reproduced from J.C. Ryle, *The Upper Room* (Wm. Hunt & Co.,

Thus far, the point to be made is not about fearing the wiles of the devil. You must fear the Lord.[5] Fearing the Lord does not mean to have a distrustful terror of God. You must fear God because He is absolutely sovereign, He is holy, He is the creator, and He is the judge.

As the sovereign creator and judge of all things, He has the power to destroy both the body and soul in hell (Matt. 10:28). In the Bible, Christians are commanded to worship Him with reverence (Heb. 12:28-29), and in spirit and in truth (John 4:24). Take time to examine the Book of Proverbs to see why it is imperative that you fear the Lord:

> My son, if you receive my words,
> And treasure my commands within you,
> So that you incline your ear to wisdom,
> And apply your heart to understanding;
> Yes, if you cry out for discernment,
> And lift up your voice for understanding,
> If you seek her as silver,
> And search for her as for hidden treasures;
> **Then you will understand the fear of the LORD,**
> And find the knowledge of God.
> For the LORD gives wisdom;
> From His mouth come knowledge and understanding
> (Prov. 2:1-6; emphasis mine).

> Do not be wise in your own eyes;
> **Fear the LORD and depart from evil**
> (Prov. 3:7; emphasis mine).

1888). I do not endorse Ryle's writings because I do not believe he preached the true gospel. Nonetheless, the excerpt I provided from Ryle makes a valid point.

[5] Fearing the Lord cannot earn merit or favor with God, nor should it be regarded as assurance of salvation. This is a gift from God that is given to the elect after they have been regenerated.

The fear of the LORD is to hate evil;
Pride and arrogance and the evil way
And the perverse mouth I hate
(Prov. 8:13; emphasis mine).

The fear of the LORD is the beginning of wisdom,
And the knowledge of the Holy One is understanding
(Prov. 9:10; emphasis mine).

The fear of the LORD prolongs days,
But the years of the wicked will be shortened
(Prov. 10:27; emphasis mine).

A wise man fears and departs from evil,
But a fool rages and is self-confident
(Prov. 14:16; emphasis mine).

In the fear of the LORD there is strong confidence,
And His children will have a place of refuge.
The fear of the LORD is a fountain of life,
To turn one away from the snares of death
(Prov. 14:26-27; emphasis mine).

Better is a little with the fear of the LORD,
Than great treasure with trouble
(Prov. 15:16; emphasis mine).

In mercy and truth
Atonement is provided for iniquity;
And by the fear of the LORD one departs from evil
(Prov. 16:6; emphasis mine).

By humility and the fear of the LORD
Are riches and honor and life
(Prov. 22:4; emphasis mine).

Do not let your heart envy sinners,
But be zealous for the fear of the LORD all the day
(Prov. 23:17; emphasis mine).

Charm is deceitful and beauty is passing,
But a woman who fears the LORD, she shall be praised
(Prov. 31:30; emphasis mine).

According to the Book of Proverbs, "The fear of the LORD is the beginning of knowledge: but fools despise wisdom and instruction" (1:7). Additionally, in Christ are hid all the treasures of wisdom and knowledge (Col. 2:3). This means that you can never have wisdom unless you appeal and submit to God in all matters of faith and practice.

Without God, you cannot make sense of the world around you. Additionally, you will have no justification for anything in this life. Christians must never abandon the biblical worldview, or embrace neutrality with anyone who does *not* submit to God as the ultimate standard of all standards. Christ explained why in Matthew 12:30: "He who is not with Me is against Me, and he who does not gather with Me scatters abroad." To know more about why it is important to fear the Lord, it is imperative that you study His attributes. *The Westminster Longer Catechism* (Question 7) provides a wonderful example:

Question: What is God?
Answer: God is a Spirit (John 4:24), in and of himself infinite in being (Exod. 3:14), glory (Acts 7:2), blessedness (1 Tim. 6:15), and perfection (Matt. 5:48); all-sufficient (Gen. 17:1), eternal (Ps. 90:2), unchangeable (Mal. 3:6), incomprehensible (1 Kings 8:27), every-where present (Ps. 139:1-13), almighty (Rev. 4:8), knowing all things (Heb. 4:13), most wise (Rom. 16:27), most holy (Is. 6:3), most just (Deut. 32:4), most merciful and gracious, long-suffering, and abundant in goodness and truth (Exod. 34:6).

Young man, do not be the fool who despises wisdom and instruction. If you do, you will be an unarmed soldier in a battlefield called *life* with no weapons to defend yourself. You will be subject to the perils of this world. You will also fall prey to the *roaring lion* that is always looking for someone to devour (1 Pet. 5:8-9). "Be not wise in your own eyes: fear the LORD, and depart from evil" (Prov. 3:7). Departing from evil is easier said than done. But if you are truly walking with the Lord, the Spirit will lead you away from evil.

Fear God and arm yourself for battle (Eph. 6:11-16). This is the only way to resist the devil (Jam. 4:7), and depart from evil. However, if you choose to be wise in your own eyes, and you think it's okay for you to live the way you want, you will be subject to prison, or eternal separation from God.

You may fool your parents, your friends, your co-workers, and your classmates with your outward display of righteousness, but you will not fool God. Unlike all of these aforementioned individuals who can only see your outward appearance, "God looks on the heart" (1 Sam. 16:7). Flee from the wicked things of the world, and fear the Lord. Look to the righteousness of Christ, which is the only grounds of justification, and assurance of salvation. I will be praying for you, my son. I love you very much. Never forget that!

CHAPTER II.
MY SON, VALUE WISDOM & INTEGRITY

God's children are neither madmen nor fools; it is but a scandal cast upon them by the madmen of the world. They are the only wise men if it be well considered. First, they make the highest end their aim, which is to be children of God here, and saints hereafter in heaven. Secondly, they aim to be found wise men at their death, and therefore are always making their accounts ready. Thirdly, they labor to live answerable to the rule; they observe the rule of the Word to be governed continually by it. Fourthly, they improve all advantages to advance their grand end; they labor to grow better by blessings and crosses, and to make a sanctified use of all things. Fifthly, they swim against the stream of the times and though they eat and drink and sleep as other men, yet (like the stars) they have a secret settled course of their own which the world cannot discern; therefore a man must be changed and set in a higher rank before he can have a sanctified judgment of the ways of God.

—Richard Sibbes

My precious son, you must understand the necessity of being wise. It is not a false dichotomy to argue that you must either be wise, or you will be a fool. Being wise is not a suggestion; it is a standard of life that demands your attention to detail. If you fail to be wise, you will make innumerable mistakes, and possibly suffer consequences that can affect the rest of your life.

Living in America, you are able to embrace the providence of God to enjoy your liberty. However, if you are not wise, you can easily have all of that liberty taken away. For example, if you misplace money in your respective place of employment, you could be arrested for theft or embezzlement. If you put your hands on someone—joking or not—you could be arrested for assault or battery. If you drive intoxicated or reckless, you could cause an accident, which could kill another driver. If you meet a young lady at a party, and you foolishly decide to have sex with her, you could suffer the consequences. You could get infected with a sexually transmitted disease. You could also be accused of a sex crime if the woman did not remember you the next day because she was too drunk the night you slept with her. All of these examples could lead you to prison for a long time. They are also violations of God's Word.

To be wise, you must define wisdom, understand the principles of wisdom, and practice wisdom. Only born-again Christians can fear God—which is the beginning of knowledge. Examine the wisdom from Solomon in Prov. 1:1-7:

> The proverbs of Solomon the son of David, king of Israel:
> To know wisdom and instruction,
> To perceive the words of understanding,
> To receive the instruction of wisdom,
> Justice, judgment, and equity;
> To give prudence to the simple,
> To the young man knowledge and discretion—
> A wise man will hear and increase learning,
> And a man of understanding will attain wise counsel,
> To understand a proverb and an enigma,
> The words of the wise and their riddles.
> **The fear of the LORD is the beginning of knowledge,**
> **But fools despise wisdom and instruction** (emphasis mine).

There are important reasons why fearing the Lord is the beginning of knowledge. Wisdom is not a standard that exists outside of God. If wisdom existed outside of God, then God would have a standard that He would be forced to measure up to. God measures up to no one. He is the standard of all standards.

Additionally, God did not create wisdom. Biblically, if God created something, He could annihilate it. Can God destroy wisdom? No! That is because God cannot destroy Himself. Wisdom is a reflection of God's eternal and divine character. Read Proverbs 8:22-31 to see why wisdom can never be regarded as a human imagination or invention:

> **The LORD possessed me at the beginning of His way,**
> **Before His works of old.**
> **I have been established from everlasting,**
> **From the beginning, before there was ever an earth.**
> **When there were no depths I was brought forth,**
> **When there were no fountains abounding with water.**
> Before the mountains were settled,
> Before the hills, I was brought forth;
> While as yet He had not made the earth or the fields,
> Or the primal dust of the world.
> **When He prepared the heavens, I was there,**
> When He drew a circle on the face of the deep,
> When He established the clouds above,
> When He strengthened the fountains of the deep,
> When He assigned to the sea its limit,
> So that the waters would not transgress His command,
> **When He marked out the foundations of the earth,**
> **Then I was beside Him as a master craftsman;**
> **And I was daily His delight,**
> Rejoicing always before Him,
> Rejoicing in His inhabited world,
> And my delight was with the sons of men
> (emphasis mine).

After examining Proverbs 8, you will see that wisdom is an attribute of God. Therefore, wisdom is always true, because God is always true. Wisdom does not contradict itself, because God does not contradict Himself. Wisdom cannot be destroyed, because God cannot be destroyed. And wisdom does not change, because God does not change. God ordained all things (Prov. 16:4, 33), and He works all things according to the counsel of His will (Eph. 1:11). The Book of Proverbs explains the value of wisdom that I pray you will read:

> **My son, if you receive my words,**
> **And treasure my commands within you,**
> So that you incline your ear to wisdom,
> And apply your heart to understanding;
> **Yes, if you cry out for discernment,**
> **And lift up your voice for understanding,**
> **If you seek her as silver,**
> **And search for her as for hidden treasures;**
> **Then you will understand the fear of the LORD,**
> And find the knowledge of God. For the LORD gives wisdom;
> From His mouth come knowledge and understanding;
> He stores up sound wisdom for the upright;
> **He is a shield to those who walk uprightly;**
> **He guards the paths of justice,**
> **And preserves the way of His saints.**
> Then you will understand righteousness and justice,
> Equity and every good path
> (Prov. 2:1-9; emphasis mine).

> My son, let them not depart from your eyes—
> Keep sound wisdom and discretion;
> So they will be life to your soul
> And grace to your neck.
> Then you will walk safely in your way,
> And your foot will not stumble.
> **When you lie down, you will not be afraid;**
> **Yes, you will lie down and your sleep will be sweet**
> (Prov. 3:21-24; emphasis mine).

> Hear, my son, and receive my sayings,
> **And the years of your life will be many...**
> Take firm hold of instruction, do not let go;
> Keep her, for she is your life
> (Prov. 4:10, 13; emphasis mine).

My son, keep your father's command,
And do not forsake the law of your mother.
Bind them continually upon your heart;
Tie them around your neck.
When you roam, they will lead you;
When you sleep, they will keep you;
And when you awake, they will speak with you.
For the commandment is a lamp,
And the law a light;
Reproofs of instruction are the way of life
(Prov. 6:20-23; emphasis mine).

Unregenerate men and women (non-Christian) will teach that being wise is a relative argument. What does relativism mean? Liberals will say, "What is right for me is right for me, and what is right for you is right to you." Clearly, this cannot account for wisdom. Unbelievers have no ultimate standard to determine the definition of wisdom. Therefore, if unbelievers are given the liberty to determine wisdom for themselves—their definition of wisdom is not wisdom at all. This is due to the fact that everyone will not agree with each other and all are capable of lies and error.

Unbelievers will also argue that the culture is what determines wisdom and truth, but this argument has no justification. Consider the following illustration to see my point:

Pastor John Doe had a conversation with a liberal, African American lady, who believed that her parents were mistreated back in the 1960s due to the color of their skin. During this conversation, Pastor Doe showed compassion for her. But when Pastor Doe opened his Bible to explain why racism is wrong, the liberal woman became upset with him. The liberal woman was upset because she felt that he should not use the Bible, exclaiming that it would require him to tell people they were wrong, and make arguments to prove that he was right. This liberal woman also argued that truth is determined by the *culture*, and by the current *laws* that govern them.

Immediately, Pastor Doe asked the liberal woman, "If that is the case, how can you say that racism was wrong back in the 1960s? During that time, the *laws* determined racism to be acceptable, and that is what the *culture* accepted."

This is what happens when people are wise in their own eyes. Examine the following Bible verses to see why being wise in yourself is dangerous:

Do not be wise in your own eyes;
Fear the LORD and depart from evil
(Prov. 3:7).

There is a way that seems right to a man,
But its end is the way of death
(Prov. 16:25).

Every way of a man is right in his own eyes,
But the LORD weighs the hearts
(Prov. 21:2).

He who trusts in his own heart is a fool,
But whoever walks wisely will be delivered
(Prov. 28:26).

My dear son, being wise requires an important word that you must be able to define, defend, and declare. It is called *integrity*. Most commonly, you will hear integrity defined as this: To do what is right—legally and morally—when no one is looking. I can agree with this definition as long as I make it clear that what is right is determined by appealing to the Bible, which can justify what is right and wrong.

If you value integrity, before you act or espouse something, you must ask yourself: "Am I honoring God with my speech or conduct?" When you are tempted by so-called friends to be mischievous, you must think twice before you partake in their actions. If you are tempted by a woman, you must remember how the Book of Proverbs provides all of the warnings about following adulterous women. Even if it costs you friends, employment, or your popularity, do not be unwise. Please understand that your actions have consequences. According to Prov. 10:9, "**He who walks with integrity walks securely, but he who perverts his ways will become known**" (emphasis mine).

My baby boy, I don't care if you have wealth, a fancy car, a high-paying job, a nice home, a lot of friends, or an *Ivy League* education. All of these things are temporal, and cannot save you. I would rather you be a born-again Christian and have nothing in this world, than for you to be wealthy and without Christ:

> **Better is the poor who walks in his integrity**
> Than one who is perverse in his lips, and is a fool
> (Prov. 19:1; emphasis mine).

> **The righteous man walks in his integrity;**
> **His children are blessed after him**
> (Prov. 20:7; emphasis mine).

> **Better is the poor who walks in his integrity**
> Than one perverse in his ways, though he be rich
> (Prov. 28:6; emphasis mine).

My son, you live in a wicked world. Satan will try desperately to sift you like wheat, and he will try to tempt you to do wicked things. If you break the law, you could be sentenced to jail or to prison, or you could harm someone or yourself. You could also bring reproach upon Christ because of your actions. Don't just fret over the things that can only take away your liberty or your life. Fear the Lord—who has the power to destroy both body and soul in hell. Be wise, fear the Lord, value wisdom and integrity.[6] Most importantly, look to the righteousness of Christ. I love you, baby boy. Do not ever forget that.

---

[6] Fearing the Lord, valuing wisdom, and embracing integrity cannot earn merit or favor with God, nor should they be regarded as assurance of salvation. Nonetheless, they are important doctrines that must be taught.

CHAPTER III.
MY SON, STAY AWAY FROM WORLDLY THINGS

> Worldliness proposes objectives which demand no radical breach with man's fallen nature; it judges the importance of things by the present and material results; it weighs success by numbers; it covets human esteem and wants no unpopularity; it knows no truth for which it is worth suffering; it declines to be a 'fool for Christ's sake.'
>
> –Iain Murray

My son, this world we live in is full of wonderful opportunities to glorify God, but it's also filled with many deadly traps called *worldliness*, which has the power to snatch you and the ones you love away.[7] I would define *worldliness* as the present world we live in—*Satan's kingdom* (John 16:11)—which will deceive you with riches, sexual pleasure, power, entertainment, self-preservation, popularity, and temporal happiness. All of these worldly traps cannot save you; on the contrary, they will condemn you. This food is poison—made in a restaurant called *hell*—and served by a waiter named Satan.

I once heard a quote from a man who said that the devil does not come dressed up like a large, red demon, with horns on his head and a long tail. Satan is too smart for that. Predators in the wild will disguise themselves, stalk, and wait patiently to ambush and kill their prey. Satan will do the same. Additionally, wounded animals in the wild don't last very long, and are subject to be killed by predators. Their ability to defend themselves is weakened because of their wounds. Likewise, young men who are struggling

---

[7] Christians can and will stumble into grievous sin, but this does not mean that one can lose their salvation. Absolutely not! True Christians can never lose their salvation because Christ infallibly secured their salvation. Therefore, this book advocates for the perseverance of the saints.

with worldliness are no different than the wounded animal. They are wounded by their love for worldliness that leaves them defenseless from Satan's attacks. I often tell young men who crave worldliness—be careful what you desire—you will eventually find it. Satan never turns anyone away. He welcomes all! Carefully heed the warning by the apostle John:

> Do not love the world or the things in the world. If anyone loves the world, the love of the Father is not in him. For all that is in the world—the lust of the flesh, the lust of the eyes, and the pride of life—is not of the Father but is of the world. And the world is passing away, and the lust of it; but he who does the will of God abides forever (1 John 2:15-17).

After examining these verses, it is imperative that you understand that worldliness is lawless, hazardous, deceptive, and perilous. First, if you crave and accept worldliness, you are craving and accepting the things that God has commanded you not to love. Therefore, it is lawless. In fact, Proverbs 8:13-25 teaches that the "fear of the Lord is to hate evil":

> **The fear of the LORD is to hate evil**;
> Pride and arrogance and the evil way
> And the perverse mouth I hate.
> Counsel is mine, and sound wisdom;
> I am understanding, I have strength.
> By me kings reign,
> And rulers decree justice.
> By me princes rule, and nobles,
> All the judges of the earth.
> I love those who love me,
> And those who seek me diligently will find me.
> Riches and honor are with me,
> Enduring riches and righteousness.
> My fruit is better than gold, yes, than fine gold,
> And my revenue than choice silver.

I traverse the way of righteousness,
In the midst of the paths of justice,
That I may cause those who love me to inherit wealth,
That I may fill their treasuries.
"The LORD possessed me at the beginning of His way,
Before His works of old.
I have been established from everlasting,
From the beginning, before there was ever an earth.
When there were no depths I was brought forth,
When there were no fountains abounding with water.
Before the mountains were settled,
Before the hills, I was brought forth (emphasis mine).

Second, worldliness is hazardous to your soul. If you love the things of the world that God has explicitly commanded you not to love, you are sending a message to God that His Word means nothing to you. Don't forget that it "is a fearful thing to fall into the hands of the living God" (Heb. 10:31).

Peer pressure is tough. It is not popular today to hang out with true Christian friends who would rather read the Word of God than to do the following:

- Go out to night clubs.
- Spend countless hours on cell phones.
- Watch filthy movies that have no regard for blaspheming God's name or citing coarse language that He hates.

Read James 4:4 to see why worldliness is hazardous: "Adulterers and adulteresses! **Do you not know that friendship with the world is enmity with God? Whoever therefore wants to be a friend of the world makes himself an enemy of God"** (emphasis mine).

Third, worldliness is deceptive. As stated earlier, Satan does not come dressed like a demon, but will come dressed like all of the things that you envy or lust over. If you are struggling with impure sexual thoughts, it does you no good to turn on your television, computer, or cell phone. You will not have to go far to see sexual perversion being exploited or flaunted on those worldly devices. Take the advice from the psalmist: "**I will set nothing wicked before my eyes**; I hate the work of those who fall away; It shall not cling to me" (Ps. 101:3; emphasis mine).

This is how the devil will tempt you: The lust of the flesh, the lust of the eyes, and the pride of life. What do these three things mean? (1) Those who struggle with sexual thoughts every time they look at a woman are being deceived by the lust of the eyes. (2) Young men who masturbate are being deceived by the lust of the flesh. (3) Carnal men who boast about possessions or accomplishments are being deceived by the pride of life.

Who is the example we can follow when we are tempted by the lust of the eyes, the lust of the flesh, and the pride of life? Examine the highlighted text in Matthew 4:1-11 to see how Jesus responded to the devil when he tried to tempt Him with the lust of the eyes ("command these stones become bread"), the lust of the flesh ("throw yourself down"), and the pride of life ("fall down and worship me"):

Then Jesus was led up by the Spirit into the wilderness to be tempted by the devil. And when He had fasted forty days and forty nights, afterward He was hungry. Now when the tempter came to Him, he said, "If You are the Son of God, command that these stones become bread." But He answered and said, "It is written, '**Man shall not live by bread alone, but by every word that proceeds from the mouth of God.**'"
Then the devil took Him up into the holy city, set Him on the pinnacle of the temple, and said to Him, "If You are the Son of God, throw Yourself down. For it is written: 'He shall give His angels charge over you,' and, 'In their hands they shall

bear you up, Lest you dash your foot against a stone.'" Jesus said to him, "It is written again, '**You shall not tempt the LORD your God**.'" Again, the devil took Him up on an exceedingly high mountain, and showed Him all the kingdoms of the world and their glory. And he said to Him, "All these things I will give You if You will fall down and worship me." Then Jesus said to him, "**Away with you, Satan! For it is written, 'You shall worship the LORD your God, and Him only you shall serve**.'" Then the devil left Him, and behold, angels came and ministered to Him.

Jesus responded with Scripture. This is how you must respond as well. Consider the following passages that relate to the topic of combatting worldliness:

Do not lay up for yourselves treasures on earth, where moth and rust destroy and where thieves break in and steal; but lay up for yourselves treasures in heaven, where neither moth nor rust destroys and where thieves do not break in and steal. For where your treasure is, there your heart will be also (Matt. 6:19-21).

I beseech you therefore, brethren, by the mercies of God, that you present your bodies a living sacrifice, holy, acceptable to God, which is your reasonable service. **And do not be conformed to this world, but be transformed by the renewing of your mind, that you may prove what *is* that good and acceptable and perfect will of God** (Rom. 12:1-2; emphasis mine).

If then you were raised with Christ, seek those things which are above, where Christ is, sitting at the right hand of God. **Set your mind on things above, not on things on the earth** (Col. 3:1-2; emphasis mine).

For the grace of God that brings salvation has appeared to all men, teaching us that, **denying ungodliness and worldly**

lusts, we should live soberly, righteously, and godly in the present age (Tit. 2:11-12; emphasis mine).

Additionally, pay careful attention to John Calvin's insightful exposition on the difficulties of battling the flesh, and the benefits of living for Christ:

> In another passage, Paul gives a brief, indeed, but more distinct account of each of the parts of a well-ordered life: "The grace of God that bringeth salvation hath appeared to all men, teaching us that, denying ungodliness and worldly lusts, we should live soberly, righteously, and godly, in this present world; looking for that blessed hope, and the glorious appearance of the great God and our Saviour Jesus Christ; who gave himself for us, that he might redeem us from all iniquity, and purify to himself a peculiar people, zealous of good works" (Tit. 2:11-14). After holding forth the grace of God to animate us, and pave the way for His true worship, he removes the two greatest obstacles which stand in the way—viz. ungodliness, to which we are by nature too prone, and worldly lusts, which are of still greater extent. Under *ungodliness*, he includes not merely superstition, but everything at variance with the true fear of God. *Worldly lusts* are equivalent to the lusts of the flesh. Thus he enjoins us, in regard to both tables of the Law, to lay aside our own mind, and renounce whatever our own reason and will dictate. Then he reduces all the actions of our lives to three branches, sobriety, righteousness, and godliness. *Sobriety* undoubtedly denotes as well chastity and temperance as the pure and frugal use of temporal goods, and patient endurance of want. *Righteousness* comprehends all the duties of equity, in every one his due. Next follows *godliness*, which separates us from the pollutions of the world, and connects us with God in true holiness. These, when connected together by an indissoluble chain, constitute complete perfection. **But as nothing is more difficult than to bid adieu to the will of the flesh, subdue, nay, abjure our lusts, devote ourselves to God and our brethren, and lead an angelic life amid the pollutions of the**

world, Paul, to set our minds free from all entanglements, recalls us to the hope of a blessed immortality, justly urging us to contend, because as Christ has once appeared as our Redeemer, so on his final advent he will give full effect to the salvation obtained by him. And in this way he dispels all the allurements which becloud our path, and prevent us from aspiring as we ought to heavenly glory; nay, he tells us that we must be pilgrims in the world, that we may not fail of obtaining the heavenly inheritance (emphasis mine).[8]

Moreover, worldliness draws men to be lovers of money, and misleads them into believing that money is the root of all happiness. My son, you must not be enticed to be a lover of money. Living in this world, you may be deceived into thinking that money is everything. Sure, you have to obtain money to buy a car, a home, pay your bills, and buy food. There may be times in life that you will have to endure financial hardships, but remember that God will provide for you: Let your conduct be without covetousness; **be content with such things as you have.** For He Himself has said, "**I will never leave you nor forsake you**" (Heb. 13:5; emphasis mine).

There are several ways the devil will try to tempt you with money. Typically, young men who were raised in low income homes will be drawn to be lovers of money, especially if they remember all of the struggles they had as a kid. Financial hardships or coveting nice things is another issue that will cause young men to lust for greed, or consider plotting ways to obtain money, which may involve illegal activity. For example, if you turn on the news, you will see that many young men have committed the following offenses:

---

[8] John Calvin, *Institutes of the Christian Religion.* Translated by Henry Beveridge. (Hendrickson Publishers, 2009), III.vii.3; emphasis mine. All subsequent references will be cited as Calvin, Institutes, III vii. 3 [for example].

- They are embezzling money from their employers.
- They are mishandling other people's money.
- They are manipulating their taxes to receive more income at the end of the year.
- They will find creative ways to cheat others out of their income so they can have personal gain.

This is why so many men are in jail or prison today. When young men become lovers of money, they will create a god out of it. They will work relentlessly to have nice things at the cost of missing invaluable family time. Mischievous young men will plan ways to obtain everything they desire, but have no regard for their own soul.

Do not forget what Christ said in Matthew 6:24: "No one can serve two masters; **for either he will hate the one and love the other, or else he will be loyal to the one and despise the other**. You cannot serve God and mammon" (emphasis mine). Therefore, do not fall for Satan's traps! Money can cause men to do wicked things. That is why you must not be a lover of money, and you must not allow money to subdue you. Paul explains why:

> But those who desire to be rich fall into temptation and a snare, and into many foolish and harmful lusts which drown men in destruction and perdition. For the love of money is a root of all kinds of evil, for which some have strayed from the faith in their greediness, and pierced themselves through with many sorrows (1 Tim. 6:9-10).

Young men who struggle with the love of money will never be satisfied. They will always want more. Read Ecclesiastes 5:10-12:

> **He who loves silver will not be satisfied with silver;**
> **Nor he who loves abundance, with increase.**
> This also is vanity.
> When goods increase,

They increase who eat them;
So what profit have the owners
Except to see them with their eyes?
The sleep of a laboring man is sweet,
Whether he eats little or much;
But the abundance of the rich will not permit him to sleep
(emphasis mine).

My son, it is better to go through life as a poor man who has God than to be a rich man without Him. What good is it if you have gained the whole world, but lose your soul (Mark 8:36)? Besides, money cannot buy everything. If you listen to the devil, and you follow your sinful desires to be wealthy, I must inform you now that money cannot buy you a godly wife, nor can it buy you a happy home that honors Christ, nor can it buy you salvation. This is why you must be content with what you have. You should focus on making memories, not money. Live your life for God, not greed.

Worldliness is perilous. My precious son, remember what the apostle John said: "The world is passing away, and the lust of it…" Everything the world offers is only temporary. Are you willing to enjoy the things of the world now and spend an eternity surrounded by the miseries of hell? Popularity, sexual pleasure, entertainment, and pride are only temporary. Remember what Christ said in Matthew 16:26: "For what profit is it to a man if he gains the whole world, and loses his own soul? Or what will a man give in exchange for his soul?"

Beware of false teachers who will decry my advice to you as legalistic. Please know that I am not telling you to perform good works to be saved. That is impossible. Good works have never saved one soul from hell, and never will. Our works can only merit the Father's wrath, and never His favor. The righteousness of Christ is the only grounds of justification and assurance of salvation. But this does not mean that you can insolently disregard the Word of God, and take every command and call it "legalistic." Notice the difference between the psalmist and the false teachers who will tell you that it is okay to live worldly: The psalmist said, "Oh, how I love Your law! It is my meditation all the day" (119:97), whereas false teachers will say, "legalism."

Please, my son, put away worldly things. Do not *waste* your life by hanging out with worldly people, or daydreaming about worldly things. You must despise worldliness.[9] If you publicly despise worldliness, you will endure the following:

- You will lose popularity.
- You will not be invited to certain places.
- You will not be liked by certain girls.
- You will be called names.
- You could also be ostracized and denied employment because of your convictions.

Nonetheless, it would be better for you to be publicly shamed and have God on your side than it would be for you to have popularity, and God against you. If you suffer because of your biblical convictions, you should rejoice. Never forget the words of the Savior: "If the world hates you, you know that it hated Me before it hated you. If you were of the world, the world would love its own. **Yet because you are not of the world, but I chose you out of the world, therefore the world hates you**" (John 15:18-19; emphasis mine).

My son, I do not care if you have nice things, or if you go to a reputable college, or if you make a lot of money, or if you have a nice home and fancy car. I only care about the following: Do you

---

[9] Despising worldliness is not a condition of salvation, nor does it provide assurance of salvation. Nonetheless, preaching against worldliness is important.

know and believe the true gospel? Are you walking with the Lord? Are you willing to die for Christ? How do you plan to serve God? Set your mind on the Word, not the world. Look to the Savior's righteousness, not self-righteousness. I love you, my son.

CHAPTER IV.
MY SON, CHOOSE YOUR FRIENDS WISELY

If any occupation or association is found to hinder our communion with God or our enjoyment of spiritual things, then it must be abandoned. Beware of 'leprosy' in the garment (Lev. 13:47). Anything in my habits or ways which mars happy fellowship with the brethren or robs me of power in service, is to be unsparingly judged and made an end of 'burned' (Lev.13:52). Whatever I cannot do for God's glory must be avoided.

—Arthur W. Pink

My son, as your parent, it is important that you understand why it is wrong and neglectful for parents to allow their children to spend time with their unbelieving friends. Parents have a responsibility to raise their children with biblical principles.

God's Word teaches that parents must train their children (biblically)—so when they are old—they will not depart from it (Prov. 22:6). Parents must also show their children what it looks like to live for Christ by being the example to them.

There are several reasons why it is appalling and neglectful when parents allow their children to spend time with their unbelieving friends.[10]

When professing Christian parents allow their children to spend time with their unbelieving friends, they are sending a message to their children and to the world that they are okay with their children walking in the counsel of the ungodly and standing

---

[10] Having compromising fellowship with an unbeliever does not mean that one is not saved, or that one can lose their salvation. Therefore, true Christians should judge one's salvation by the gospel they profess. Nonetheless, the Bible warns about compromising fellowship.

in the way of sinners. Read Psalm 1:1-2 to see why these kinds of parents desperately need reformation in their parenting:

> **Blessed is the man**
> **Who walks not in the counsel of the ungodly,**
> **Nor stands in the path of sinners,**
> **Nor sits in the seat of the scornful**;
> But his delight is in the law of the LORD,
> And in His law he meditates day and night
> (emphasis mine).

Parents who allow their children to spend time with their unbelieving friends are guilty of the following:

- They have forfeited precious time that God has given them with their children.
- They have provided unbelievers with opportunities to influence their children with their godless worldviews.
- They have taken a dangerous risk of allowing their children's minds to be corrupted by others who embrace the world, and not the Word.

These kinds of parents have grossly neglected their responsibility to raise their children in the admonition and discipline in the Lord. These kinds of parents are not leading their children to the Savior; on the contrary, they are delivering them over to Satan.

I was once friends with a man who complained to others that his child wandered from the faith, but failed to mention that he was the one who allowed his child to spend lots of time with his unbelieving friends who despise the gospel. After confronted with the fact that his child was godless, this father said, "I am just going to give my rebellious child to the Lord." This father did not give his child to the Lord; he handed his child over to Satan long ago.

This is what happens when parents disregard 1 Cor. 15:33 which states, "Bad company corrupts good morals."

Young men must be taught about the dangers of having compromising fellowship with unbelievers. Consider the warning by Matthew Henry:

> But, having confuted their principle, he now warns the Corinthians how dangerous such men's conversation must prove. **He tells them that they would probably be corrupted by them, and fall in with their course of life, if they gave into their evil principles. Note, Bad company and conversation are likely to make bad men. Those who would keep their innocence must keep good company**. Error and vice are infectious: and, if we would avoid the contagion, we must keep clear of those who have taken it. *He that walketh with wise men shall be wise; but a companion of fools shall be destroyed* (Prov. 13:20 emphasis mine).[11]

There are parents who will allow their children to associate with unbelieving friends, which blatantly disregards the teachings of Scripture. There are usually three reasons why parents allow their children to associate with unbelievers:

- First, they may have a personal bias, or they are busy with work.
- Second, they submit to their children's continual pressure.
- Third, they have no ability to lead their homes biblically.
- Therefore, they allow their children to associate with whomever they want, and neglect what God commands.

Parents who allow this to happen are not victims of rogue children who will not listen. These parents are guilty of spiritual

---

[11] Matthew Henry, *Commentary on the Whole Bible*. VOL. VI. Acts to Revelation (New York: Fleming H. Revell Company), 502-593. This excerpt by Henry is from his commentary on First Corinthians 15:33.

child abuse for allowing their children to fall prey to all of the devil's habits. When children have adopted bad habits from their unbelieving friends, it's not uncommon to hear parents complain that their children are in open rebellion against God. This is what happens when children desire to associate with unbelieving friends, and biblically ignorant parents allow it.

As a child, you must understand that there is absolutely no benefit whatsoever for you to associate with unbelievers. An unbelieving and worldly child who associates with another unbelieving and worldly child will never produce a wise man.

If you were a mature Christian, you would be commanded to be around worldly people, not to have a compromising relationship with them, but to preach Christ to their hearts. As a child, you need to be disciplined by godly parents who will teach you the gospel and how to live for Christ. Having fellowship with unbelievers will only indoctrinate you with ungodly principles that will pervert what you have been taught thus far. Consider Paul's warning in 1 Corinthians 5:9-11:

> I wrote to you in my epistle not to keep company with sexually immoral people. **Yet I certainly did not mean with the sexually immoral people of this world, or with the covetous, or extortioners, or idolaters, since then you would need to go out of the world**. But now I have written to you not to keep company with anyone named a brother, who is sexually immoral, or covetous, or an idolater, or a reviler, or a drunkard, or an extortioner—not even to eat with such a person (emphasis mine).

Notice how Paul said, "...since then you would need to go out of the world." Paul is not commanding the church to isolate themselves from *all contact* with people in the world who are sexually immoral. If this were the case, evangelism would be impossible. This would have prohibited Christians from interacting with *all* sexually immoral people. You must avoid the notion that Paul is prohibiting the church in 1 Corinthians 5:9 from associating with all wicked people in the world.

Paul clarified his position on not associating with sexually immoral people (v. 11). The apostle referred to those who call themselves "a brother" (i.e., a Christian). Put another way, Christians are not to associate with those who profess to be Christians, but live like impenitent devils.

Paul commanded the church to not associate with those who profess Christianity, but are sexually immoral. The apostle also enumerated on several other sins (greed, idolatry, revilement, drunkenness, and fraud) that will lead impenitent sinners down the unbridled path towards hell.

The Bible also commands Christians to not have compromising fellowship with worldly individuals. The Book of Proverbs provides a few examples to study:

> He who walks with wise men will be wise,
> But the companion of fools will be destroyed
> (Prov. 13:20).

> Go from the presence of a foolish man,
> When you do not perceive in him the lips of knowledge
> (Prov. 14:7).

> He who goes about as a talebearer reveals secrets;
> Therefore do not associate with one who flatters with his lips
> (Prov. 20:19).

Do not be envious of evil men,
Nor desire to be with them
(Prov. 24:1).

My son, do not have fellowship with those who despise the Word of God. Witness to the lost, but do not compromise. There are several reasons why you should witness to unbelievers, but never have fellowship with them:

- Unbelievers do not appeal and submit to God's Word.
- Unbelievers despise the gospel of Christ.
- Unbelievers embrace sexual immorality.
- Unbelievers will use the Lord's name in vain.
- Unbelievers embrace the murder of children (abortion).
- Unbelievers will lavish all of the things that God hates.
- Unbelievers use vile language, and they love strife.

Do not follow in their paths! Run from them! Follow the warnings from Proverbs 1:8-19:

My son, hear the instruction of your father,
And do not forsake the law of your mother;
For they will be a graceful ornament on your head,
And chains about your neck.
My son, if sinners entice you,
Do not consent.
If they say, "Come with us,
Let us lie in wait to shed blood;
Let us lurk secretly for the innocent without cause;
Let us swallow them alive like Sheol,
And whole, like those who go down to the Pit;
We shall find all kinds of precious possessions,
We shall fill our houses with spoil;
Cast in your lot among us,
Let us all have one purse"—
My son, do not walk in the way with them,
Keep your foot from their path;

For their feet run to evil,
And they make haste to shed blood.
Surely, in vain the net is spread
In the sight of any bird;
But they lie in wait for their own blood,
They lurk secretly for their own lives.
So are the ways of everyone who is greedy for gain;
It takes away the life of its owners (emphasis mine).

My beloved son, there is a great storm coming, and it is called *the judgment of God*. Do not have compromising fellowship with unbelievers. Examine Proverbs 1:25-33 to see why this is important:

Because you disdained all my counsel,
And would have none of my rebuke,
I also will laugh at your calamity;
I will mock when your terror comes,
When your terror comes like a storm,
And your destruction comes like a whirlwind,
When distress and anguish come upon you.
"Then they will call on me, but I will not answer;
They will seek me diligently, but they will not find me.
Because they hated knowledge
And did not choose the fear of the LORD,
They would have none of my counsel
And despised my every rebuke.
Therefore they shall eat the fruit of their own way,
And be filled to the full with their own fancies.
For the turning away of the simple will slay them,
And the complacency of fools will destroy them;
But whoever listens to me will dwell safely,
And will be secure, without fear of evil."

Search for friends who know the gospel, look for friends who love God's Word, and embrace friends in the local church who are committed to the person and work of Christ. Stay in prayer, read

God's Word daily, and never be wise in your own eyes. Do not be guilty by association, and avoid the appearance of evil. This is why you must "Fear the Lord and turn away from evil" (Prov. 3:7). I love you, son.

CHAPTER V.
MY SON, RUN FROM SEXUAL SIN

Satan's time of tempting is usually after an ordinance; and the reason is, because then he thinks he shall find us most secure. When we have been at solemn duties, we are apt to think all is done, and we grow remiss, and leave off that zeal and strictness as before; just as a soldier, who after a battle leaves off his armour, not once dreaming, of an enemy. Satan watches his time, and when we least suspect, then he throws in a temptation.

—Thomas Watson

My son, there is a time in the life of every child when their parents must talk with them about uncomfortable topics. Sexual intimacy is not the most comfortable topic for any child to talk with their parents about. Nonetheless, it is a conversation that cannot be avoided.

Since everyone has a sinful nature, every sinner is capable of abusing and creating idols out of everything. This is why I must plead with you to flee from sexual immorality. Sexual immorality can be defined in several ways:

- Having sexual relations outside of marriage (1 Cor. 7:2, 8-9; Heb. 13:4).
- Having adulterous thoughts and affections (Matt. 5:28).
- Committing shameful acts with the same sex (Rom. 1:26-27).
- Engaging in sexual relations with an animal (Lev. 20:15-16).
- Approving of those who practice all of the aforementioned things (Rom. 1:32).

Satan will tempt you to commit sexual immorality. Satan will try to deceive you with the lust of the eyes, and the lust of the flesh. What does this mean? For example, if you see an outwardly attractive woman, you may be deceived by the lust of the eyes. Once this happens, you may desire to be sexually involved with that woman to fulfill the lust of the flesh. You must flee from this. There are several reasons why having sexual thoughts is sinful.

First, Christ said in Matthew 5:28: "But I say to you that whoever looks at a woman to lust for her has already committed adultery with her in his heart." Yes, this is correct. You are committing adultery every time you think about having sexual relations with a woman.

Second, having sexually immoral thoughts is sinful. When you are drawn away by desire, it never leads to anything good. Consider the warning in James 1:14-15: "But each one is tempted when he is drawn away by his own desires and enticed. Then, when desire has conceived, it gives birth to sin; and sin, when it is full-grown, brings forth death."

My son, if you struggle with sexual thoughts, you may also struggle with masturbation. This is a sinful act that you must stay away from! Masturbation is an idol. Young men who worship this idol find pleasure in adulterous thoughts. In the bond of marriage, a man will have sexual relations with his wife to be fruitful and multiply. Marriage is not about pleasing ourselves.

According to the Bible, men will please their wives, and the wives will please their husbands. The apostle Paul provided several principles of marriage in 1 Corinthians 7:1-9:

...It is good for a man not to touch a woman. Nevertheless, because of sexual immorality, **let each man have his own wife, and let each woman have her own husband. Let the husband render to his wife the affection due her, and**

likewise also the wife to her husband. The wife does not have authority over her own body, but the husband does. And likewise the husband does not have authority over his own body, but the wife does. Do not deprive one another except with consent for a time, that you may give yourselves to fasting and prayer; and come together again so that Satan does not tempt you because of your lack of self-control. But I say this as a concession, not as a commandment. For I wish that all men were even as I myself. But each one has his own gift from God, one in this manner and another in that. But I say to the unmarried and to the widows: It is good for them if they remain even as I am; but if they cannot exercise self-control, let them marry. For it is better to marry than to burn with passion (emphasis mine).

Third, if you struggle with masturbation, you may carry out your sinful thoughts! Promiscuous women are the devil's harlots, and they are everywhere. Do not fall into this trap! Examine the Bible verses below to see the trap that Satan has set for you:

1. Adulterous women will dress provocatively—like a harlot:

And there a woman met him,
With the attire of a harlot, and a crafty heart
(Prov. 7:10).

2. Adulterous women are aggressive in their seduction:

So she caught him and kissed him…
(Prov. 7:13).

3. Adulterous women will use flattery speech to draw their victims to them:

That they may keep you from the immoral woman,
From the seductress who flatters with her words
(Prov. 7:5).

So I came out to meet you,
Diligently to seek your face,
And I have found you.
I have spread my bed with tapestry,
Colored coverings of Egyptian linen.
I have perfumed my bed
With myrrh, aloes, and cinnamon.
Come, let us take our fill of love until morning;
Let us delight ourselves with love.
For my husband is not at home;
He has gone on a long journey;
He has taken a bag of money with him,
And will come home on the appointed day."
With her enticing speech she caused him to yield,
With her flattering lips she seduced him
(Prov. 7:15-21; emphasis mine).

My beloved son, you must not fall into Satan's traps! Flee
from adulterous women. If you fall into Satan's traps, here are the
consequences:

1. You will find certain death:

For her house leads down to death,
And her paths to the dead;
None who go to her return,
Nor do they regain the paths of life
(Prov. 2:18-19).

2. Your disgrace will not be wiped away:

Whoever commits adultery with a woman lacks
understanding;
He who does so destroys his own soul.
Wounds and dishonor he will get,
And his reproach will not be wiped away
(Prov. 6:32-33).

3. You will find sexual pleasure in the bedroom of a whore—which is the trap door that leads to hell:

Do not let your heart turn aside to her ways,
Do not stray into her paths;
For she has cast down many wounded,
And all who were slain by her were strong men.
Her house is the way to hell,
Descending to the chambers of death
(Prov. 7:25-27; emphasis mine).

My precious son, you must not even put yourself in the predicament to be around worldly women. This is why you must stay away from late night parties and nightclubs. Stay away from women who are not believers. Women who do not affirm the Bible will commit sexual immorality with you, but also with others. You must abstain from all appearances of evil (1 Thess. 5:22).

Joseph is an excellent example of why you do not even want to be around worldly women. He was regarded as a good man who was well favored. Potiphar's wife cast her eyes on Joseph. This woman asked Joseph to sleep with her, but he refused (Gen. 39:7-8). This did not stop Potiphar's wife! She repeatedly asked Joseph to sleep with her, but he adamantly refused. Therefore, she plotted a great lie to accuse Joseph of sexually assaulting her, which subsequently resulted in Joseph being put into prison for a crime that he did not commit:

And it came to pass about this time, that Joseph went into the house to do his business; and there was none of the men of the house there within. **And she caught him by his garment, saying, lie with me: and he left his garment in her hand, and fled, and got him out. And it came to pass, when she saw that he had left his garment in her hand, and was fled forth, that she called unto the men of her house, and spake unto them, saying, See, he hath brought in an Hebrew unto**

us to mock us; he came in unto me to lie with me, and I cried with a loud voice: And it came to pass, when he heard that I lifted up my voice and cried, that he left his garment with me, and fled, and got him out. And she laid up his garment by her, until his lord came home. And she spake unto him according to these words, saying, The Hebrew servant, which thou hast brought unto us, came in unto me to mock me: And it came to pass, as I lifted up my voice and cried, that he left his garment with me, and fled out (Gen. 39:11-18, KJV; emphasis mine).

Joseph was innocent, yet he was accused of a crime. As a young man, don't ever put yourself in a position where one can accuse you of a crime. The warnings from Scripture should cause you to flee from immoral women. Rape and sexual assault allegations can publicly shame you for life, or take your liberty away for a long time. Most importantly, you should flee from sexually immorality because of the following:

- Sexual immorality dishonors God.
- Sexual immorality breaks God's law.
- Sexual immorality is deserving of death.
- Sexual immorality can lead you to jail or prison.

This is why you must listen to my counsel and be wise. Never put yourself in a situation where you could be tempted to commit sexual immorality. Stay far away from worldly women.

**Therefore hear me now, my children,
And do not depart from the words of my mouth.
Remove your way far from her,
And do not go near the door of her house,**
Lest you give your honor to others,
And your years to the cruel one;
Lest aliens be filled with your wealth,
And your labors go to the house of a foreigner;

And you mourn at last,
When your flesh and your body are consumed,
And say: "How I have hated instruction,
And my heart despised correction!
I have not obeyed the voice of my teachers,
Nor inclined my ear to those who instructed me!
I was on the verge of total ruin,
In the midst of the assembly and congregation"
(Prov. 5:7-14; emphasis mine).

My son, the world we live in hates God. Examine the following reasons why:

- God created male and female (Gen. 5:2), while the world accepts the delusional belief that a man can become a woman and a woman can become a man (transgenderism)
- God's Word teaches that a man will leave his mother and father and be joined to his wife (Gen. 2:24), while the world teaches that a man can leave his mother and father and be joined to his husband (homosexuality).

Those who regard sexual immorality as sin will be decried as bigots, racists, unloving, or intolerant. The wicked have no fear of God in their eyes, even though God has given plenty of warnings:

as Sodom and Gomorrah, and the cities around them in a similar manner to these, having given themselves over to sexual immorality and gone after strange flesh, **are set forth as an example, suffering the vengeance of eternal fire** (Jude 7; emphasis mine).

My beloved son, flee from sexual immorality. Stay far away from worldly women. However, abstaining from sexual immorality cannot save you. Christ perfectly obeyed the law, and He died for the elect. This is the righteousness that is the only grounds of justification, and assurance of salvation. I love you, and I pray that you will follow Paul's guidance:

> If then you were raised with Christ, seek those things which are above, where Christ is, sitting at the right hand of God. Set your mind on things above, not on things on the earth. For you died, and your life is hidden with Christ in God. When Christ who is our life appears, then you also will appear with Him in glory. Therefore put to death your members which are on the earth: fornication, uncleanness, passion, evil desire, and covetousness, which is idolatry. Because of these things the wrath of God is coming upon the sons of disobedience, in which you yourselves once walked when you lived in them. But now you yourselves are to put off all these: anger, wrath, malice, blasphemy, filthy language out of your mouth. Do not lie to one another, since you have put off the old man with his deeds, and have put on the new man who is renewed in knowledge according to the image of Him who created him, where there is neither Greek nor Jew, circumcised nor uncircumcised, barbarian, Scythian, slave nor free, but Christ is all and in all (Col. 3:1-11).

CHAPTER VI.
MY SON, CONTROL YOUR PRIDE, ANGER & MOUTH

A truly humble man is sensible of his natural distance from God; of his dependence on Him; of the insufficiency of his own power and wisdom; and that it is by God's power that he is upheld and provided for, and that he needs God's wisdom to lead and guide him, and His might to enable him to do what he ought to do for Him.

—Jonathan Edwards

My son, sin is a cancer that exists in every human being. Even though God saves sinners, every human being will still sin. Since we are all sinners, there are all types of sin that are cancerous to the soul. In this chapter, I want to warn you about three dangerous sins that every human being—saved or unsaved—need to be aware of: Pride, anger, and perverse speech.

Beware of pride

Living in a sinful world, you must be reminded that Satan is the ruler of this age. Since we live in a sinful world, we are subject to fall under the same snares of Satan, when he tempted Adam and Eve in the garden. Therefore, you must know that God hates pride (Prov. 8:13), and is adamantly against it. You must be humble in the sight of God.[12] See what James wrote concerning this matter:

But He gives more grace. Therefore He says: "**God resists the proud, but gives grace to the humble**." Therefore submit to God. Resist the devil and he will flee from you. Draw near to

---

[12] Humbling yourself cannot earn merit or favor with God. Put another way, humbling yourself is not a condition or assurance of salvation. God humbles sinners, according to His immutable will. Nonetheless, the Bible commands believers to humble themselves in the sight of God.

God and He will draw near to you. Cleanse your hands, you sinners; and purify your hearts, you double-minded. Lament and mourn and weep! Let your laughter be turned to mourning and your joy to gloom. **Humble yourselves in the sight of the Lord**, and He will lift you up (Jam. 4:6-10; emphasis mine).

Struggling with pride is a serious issue that should never be mitigated. There are several examples of pride. See the following:

- Boast in one's accomplishments.
- Take selfies (i.e., photos) of either your physique or face to show others how physically built or attractive you are.
- Never admit to being wrong or pretending to always be right.
- Speak contemptuously against the Bible, and God.
- Despise discipline and wise counsel.
- Treat others like they are less valuable than you since they have not accomplished what you have, or do not have what you possess.
- Consistently denigrate and mock others who are not like you.
- Show favoritism towards others who are esteemed by many because they have what you desire.

All of these examples of pride are dangerous. A young man may enjoy temporal happiness for a time, but will eventually be shamed, and destroyed if God does not grant that poor sinner repentance and mercy. The gospel is the antidote.

Examine the Bible, and you will see that pride is a result of the fall, when sin entered into the human race. Every time you look in the Bible, you will find out how to combat all the hellish examples of pride. When you struggle with pride, you must look to the Bible to see the examples of pride, but also the effects of it. For example, if you know men who love division, it is because they are struggling with pride since it brings "nothing but strife" (Prov.

13:10). Additionally, if you know men who act arrogantly, you may know them by their given name, but the Bible knows them by another: "A proud and haughty man—**'Scoffer'** is his name; He acts with arrogant pride" (Prov. 21:24, emphasis mine).

My son, you must fight against pride, and not let it consume you like it has so many others. If you catch yourself saying prideful things, like boasting in yourself in front of others, you must remember: "Let another man praise you, and not your own mouth; A stranger, and not your own lips" (Prov. 27:2).

Pride will creep up on you when you least expect it. At times, you will be surrounded by men that foster pride in their daily lives. "Do you see a man wise in his own eyes? There is more hope for a fool than for him" (Prov. 26:12). That is why you must be careful who you associate with. The Bible teaches that it is "better to be of a humble spirit with the lowly, than to divide the spoil with the proud" (Prov. 16:19). Therefore, do not boast in anything except the Lord:

> Thus says the LORD:
> "Let not the wise man glory in his wisdom,
> Let not the mighty man glory in his might,
> Nor let the rich man glory in his riches;
> **But let him who glories glory in this,**
> **That he understands and knows Me,**
> **That I am the LORD, exercising lovingkindness,**
> **judgment, and righteousness in the earth.**
> **For in these I delight," says the LORD**
> (Jer. 9:23-24; emphasis mine).

You must wage war against pride, but you must also warn others about its danger. A prideful heart is sinful (Prov. 21:4), shameful (Prov. 11:2), and will not go unpunished (Prov. 16:5). If you trust in self-righteousness, and not the Savior's righteousness, you will stand naked before the Lord one day and give an account to God.

Pride caused the devil to be cast out of heaven. Therefore, do not think that you cannot be cast down to the darkest pit if you embrace self-righteousness, and not the Savior's righteousness. Nothing good ever comes from pride! Pride causes men to be angry. Pride also causes angry men to say things that they will regret. You must be warned!

Control your anger

Anger can cause a young man to do many irrational and sinful things. You could either scream or threaten someone who offended you, or you could say divisive things to others who made you mad. You could also find yourself involved in an altercation, depending on how mad you become. It is not hard to cause a young man to become angry. Anger can lead you into hot water, so to speak.

There are several reasons why you must control your anger. Struggling with anger can cause others to fear you. This is not a good thing. Accosting someone who offended you could lead you into trouble. The person you accosted could feel threatened, and legally call the police on you. This means that you could be charged with a misdemeanor, or a felony. The criminal charge will be determined on what you said in anger, and how threatened the person felt. Yes, if you lose your anger, you could lose your liberty, and be incarcerated.

Displaying anger in your respective place of employment could also lead you in trouble. A bystander could file a complaint against you for causing a hostile work environment, and you could be fired from your job, which could harm your reputation. Is this how you want to be humbled? If you want to be wise, listen to the counsel of James, who said: "So then, my beloved brethren, let every man be swift to hear, slow to speak, slow to wrath; for the wrath of man does not produce the righteousness of God" (Jam. 1:19-20).

Losing your anger may also cause someone to lose their anger with you. Assaults happen all of the time in America. It is not uncommon for someone to lose their temper, and place their hands on someone who caused them to be angry. Do not think that you can lose your temper on someone and there will not be any consequences for your actions. The person you become angry with could assault you, or they could take out a firearm and shoot you or someone you are with. This is what happens when men are provoked to anger.

You must learn how to control your anger, and provide an edifying response to others, instead of an angry one. You must be wise, and remember: "A soft answer turns away wrath, but a harsh word stirs up anger" (Prov. 15:1), and "a wrathful man stirs up strife, but he who is slow to anger allays contention" (Prov. 15:18).

You need to be careful with your anger because you could provoke other Christians to anger. Christians who struggle with anger need friends who will help them, not incite them to stay angry. This is why Proverbs 22:24 states, "Make no friendship with an angry man, and with a furious man do not go."

Christians and liberals handle anger differently. Liberals vent their feelings by speaking whatever is on their mind. This is grossly wrong. Consider Proverbs 29:11 to see why: "A fool vents all his feelings, but a wise man holds them back." The Bible commands Christians to despise anger because of the harm it causes (Ps. 37:8). God's Word also teaches that Christians are to put away anger and wrath from their mouths (Col. 3:8). Young men that do not do these things are regarded as fools (Eccl. 7:9).

Watch your mouth

My beloved son, the tongue is a dangerous weapon. There are many in this life who will praise God with their lips. But with these same lips, they will curse men who were made after the similitude of God. The Apostle James declares:

> Indeed, we put bits in horses' mouths that they may obey us, and we turn their whole body. Look also at ships: although they are so large and are driven by fierce winds, they are turned by a very small rudder wherever the pilot desires. Even so the tongue is a little member and boasts great things. See how great a forest a little fire kindles! **And the tongue is a fire, a world of iniquity. The tongue is so set among our members that it defiles the whole body, and sets on fire the course of nature; and it is set on fire by hell.** For every kind of beast and bird, of reptile and creature of the sea, is tamed and has been tamed by mankind. **But no man can tame the tongue. It is an unruly evil, full of deadly poison.** With it we bless our God and Father, and with it we curse men, who have been made in the similitude of God. Out of the same mouth proceed blessing and cursing. My brethren, these things ought not to be so. Does a spring send forth fresh water and bitter from the same opening? Can a fig tree, my brethren, bear olives, or a grapevine bear figs? Thus no spring yields both salt water and fresh (Jam. 3:3-12; emphasis mine).

When you go through life, you will start to notice how dangerous the tongue is. With it, you will hear young men use foul speech, make threats, fabricate stories, joke coarsely, talk perversely to women, make racist jokes, say the Lord's name in vain, and gossip. Christ said that out of the abundance of the heart, the mouth speaks (Matt. 12:34). Christ also said that what comes out of the mouth is what defiles a man (Matt. 15:11). If you are tempted to say wicked things, you must be warned:

> A man who isolates himself seeks his own desire;
> He rages against all wise judgment.
> A fool has no delight in understanding,
> But in expressing his own heart.
> When the wicked comes, contempt comes also;
> And with dishonor comes reproach.
> The words of a man's mouth are deep waters;
> The wellspring of wisdom is a flowing brook.
> It is not good to show partiality to the wicked,
> Or to overthrow the righteous in judgment.
> **A fool's lips enter into contention,**
> **And his mouth calls for blows.**
> **A fool's mouth is his destruction,**
> **And his lips are the snare of his soul.**
> **The words of a talebearer are like tasty trifles,**
> **And they go down into the inmost body**
> (Prov. 18:1-8; emphasis mine).

> **He who passes by and meddles in a quarrel not his own**
> **Is like one who takes a dog by the ears.**
> **Like a madman who throws firebrands, arrows, and death,**
> **Is the man who deceives his neighbor,**
> **And says, "I was only joking!"**
> Where there is no wood, the fire goes out;
> **And where there is no talebearer, strife ceases.**
> As charcoal is to burning coals, and wood to fire,
> So is a contentious man to kindle strife.
> **The words of a talebearer are like tasty trifles,**
> **And they go down into the inmost body.**
> **Fervent lips with a wicked heart**
> **Are like earthenware covered with silver dross.**
> **He who hates, disguises it with his lips,**
> **And lays up deceit within himself;**
> **When he speaks kindly, do not believe him,**
> For there are seven abominations in his heart;

Though his hatred is covered by deceit,
His wickedness will be revealed before the assembly.
Whoever digs a pit will fall into it,
And he who rolls a stone will have it roll back on him.
A lying tongue hates those who are crushed by it,
And a flattering mouth works ruin
(Prov. 26:17-28; emphasis mine).

Be wise my son, and do not follow these examples. Remember that "death and life are in the power of the tongue, and those who love it will eat its fruit" (Prov. 18:21). This is why you must read Scripture every day. Reading Scripture is the only way you can be armed for battle against the wicked things that men will speak. "Set a guard, O LORD, over my mouth; keep watch over the door of my lips" (Ps. 141:3).

Do not be deceived by the power of the tongue. For example, if you receive a call at home from a telemarketer, you may ask someone who is with you to tell them that you are not home, when you were. What is the problem with this? You may deceive yourself into thinking that it is only a white lie, so to speak, without realizing that there is no such thing as a white lie. Telling white lies, fabricating stories, and exaggerating are all lies. Thus, refrain from speaking evil.

"He who would love life
And see good days,
Let him refrain his tongue from evil,
And his lips from speaking deceit"
(1 Pet. 3:10).

Be wise and remember what God's word teaches: "He who guards his mouth preserves his life, but he who opens wide his lips shall have destruction" (Prov. 13:3). The Book of Proverbs also states, "The heart of the righteous studies how to answer, but the mouth of the wicked pours forth evil" (15:28), and "whoever guards his mouth and tongue keeps his soul from troubles" (21:23).

Once you choose a profession to work in, either religious or secular, you must avoid all of the gossip and slander that comes from the workplace. When colleagues or friends approach you with gossip or slander, do not acknowledge their comments, and do not say anything. Have nothing to do with their evil. "Keep your tongue from evil, and your lips from speaking deceit" (Ps. 34:13).

Follow Paul's advice in Ephesians 4:29: "Let no corrupt word proceed out of your mouth, but what is good for necessary edification, that it may impart grace to the hearers." Young men who are wise in their own eyes will not heed the warnings from Scripture. As a result, they will speak their mind, so to speak. Lord have mercy on them. Christ said in Matthew 12:36, "But I say to you that for every idle word men may speak, they will give account of it in the day of judgment."

Closing

My son, I pray that you will listen to my advice. Young men who boast in themselves fail to see that God hates their pride. Those who display anger and speak imprudently are ignorant of all of the consequences that the Bible teaches.

Be wise and humble, my beloved son. Boast in nothing except the cross of Christ. Be angry towards sin, but do not sin with your anger. And speak evil of no one, but be peaceable, gentle, showing humility to all men (Tit. 3:2).[13] I love you, son.

---

[13] Controlling your pride, anger, and mouth are important, but they are not conditions or assurance of salvation.

CHAPTER VII.
MY SON, PRAY FOR A GODLY WIFE

Moses now relates that marriage was divinely instituted, which is especially useful to be known; for since Adam did not take a wife to himself at his own will, but received her as offered and appropriated to him by God, the sanctity of marriage hence more clearly appears, because we recognize God as its Author. The more Satan has endeavored to dishonor marriage, the more should we vindicate it from all reproach and abuse, that it may receive its due reverence.

—John Calvin

My son, you must be repeatedly warned about staying far away from sexual immorality and adulterous women. Flee from sexual sin! As a young man, you must be aware that Satan will try to attack the family unit—the bond between a man and his wife. This is why you must be wise in finding a wife who is a true Christian. According to Proverbs 18:22, "He who finds a wife finds a good thing, and obtains favor from the LORD." It is quite natural for a young man to seek a wife. Here is why:

> There comes a time in the life of a young man that he goes out to seek a life mate for himself. This is quite natural, for when God created us, He said, "It is not good that the man should be alone; I will make him an help meet for him" (Gen. 2:18). There is nothing sinful or improper about this going out to seek a mate. This natural drive may even be spiritually motivated. A serious son of the church is not merely interested in finding a mate, but realizes that he needs a companion and a helper to carry out his calling in God's church. To fulfill his Christian stewardship he needs the comfort of his own home, the help of his wife, and the intimate love and fellowship of

his family. Thus the desire to marry can be as holy as the holy institution of marriage itself.[14]

From the moment of creation, God established marriage as a holy institution between a man and a woman. God's creation ordinance of marriage is a beautiful picture of Christ, the bridegroom, uniting with his bride, the church. When a young man has reached an age of maturity, he will leave his mother and father and be joined to his wife:

> And the LORD God said, "**It is not good that man should be alone**; **I will make him a helper comparable to him**." Out of the ground the LORD God formed every beast of the field and every bird of the air, and brought them to Adam to see what he would call them. And whatever Adam called each living creature, that was its name. So Adam gave names to all cattle, to the birds of the air, and to every beast of the field. But for Adam there was not found a helper comparable to him. And the LORD God caused a deep sleep to fall on Adam, and he slept; and He took one of his ribs, and closed up the flesh in its place. Then the rib which the LORD God had taken from man He made into a woman, and He brought her to the man. And Adam said:
> "This is now bone of my bones
> And flesh of my flesh;
> She shall be called Woman,
> Because she was taken out of Man."
> **Therefore a man shall leave his father and mother and be joined to his wife, and they shall become one flesh** (Gen. 2:18-24; emphasis mine).

Finding a wife requires patience and much prayer that the Lord will deliver her to you. There are several reasons why prayer and patience are important.

---

[14] Cornelius Hanko, *Leaving Father and Mother: Biblical Courtship and Marriage*. (Grandville, MI: Reformed Free Publishing Association, 2001), 5.

Being impatient and reckless will deceive you into believing that love is defined by a standard that God has not instituted in His Word. Love is a reflection of God's attributes; therefore, love must be defined by His standard, not yours.

Do not define love by the standards of the world, which is similar to a wave being tossed by the wind. You will never know which direction the waves are heading, and where it will end. And it will always change. You do not want this kind of love in your marriage. This is why divorce is prevalent in the present culture. Therefore, it is imperative that you understand the principles of marriage.

Unconverted young women are not hard to find. They are everywhere. By their fruits you will know them:

- They do not believe in Christ's gospel.
- They are disrespectful to their parents.
- They will associate with godless friends.
- They will dress like immodest harlots.
- They will speak like devils.
- They have no desire to be godly because they crave worldly things.
- They have no regard for being submissive to their future husbands.

All of these characteristics are contrary to what is taught in God's Word. This is why you must pray for a woman who believes the gospel, and is filled with the Holy Spirit. You will be enraptured by her love:

Let your fountain be blessed,
And rejoice with the wife of your youth.
As a loving deer and a graceful doe,
Let her breasts satisfy you at all times;

And always be enraptured with her love
(Prov. 5:18-19).

First, pray for a woman who believes in the true gospel of Jesus Christ. There are many young ladies who believe in a Jesus who loves all, and died for all. This is not the Jesus of the Bible. The true Christ died for the elect, and He loves the elect.

Second, pray for a woman who honors her parents. Moses said, "Honor your father and your mother," and "He who curses father or mother, let him be put to death" (Mark 7:10). A young woman who cannot honor and show respect to her own parents will not show honor and respect to her husband. Therefore, when you are in the phase of meeting a young woman's parents, listen carefully how she speaks to her parents. This will give you a preview of the type of person that you may spend the rest of your life with. If she speaks disrespectfully and dishonorably to her parents, run, and don't look back!

Third, pray for a wife who associates with godly friends. An example of godly friends will be older women in the church who are:

> "…reverent in behavior, not slanderers, not given to much wine, teachers of good things—that they admonish the young women to love their husbands, to love their children, to be discreet, chaste, homemakers, good, obedient to their own husbands, that the word of God may not be blasphemed" (Tit. 2:3-5).

Older and wiser women in the local church are excellent examples for younger women in the faith. Immature, worldly, and unconverted women are corrupt, and they are like cancer to everyone in their path. This is why you must be wise, and pay careful attention to the type of friends that your aspiring wife associates with. Remember, 1 Corinthians 15:33 states, "Bad company corrupts good character." Therefore, if you meet a young woman, and notice that she associates with immature, worldly, and unconverted women, run, and don't look back!

Fourth, pray for a wife who dresses modestly, and fears the Lord. According to Prov. 31:30, "…a woman who fears the LORD, she shall be praised." This is the kind of woman you must seek. There are several reasons why you need to stay away from immodest women:

1. They dress no differently than prostitutes, which are described in Prov. 7:10: "…**With the attire of a harlot, and a crafty heart**" (emphasis mine).

2. They will try desperately to flaunt the most provocative parts of their body. For example, they will purposely wear tight jeans to flaunt their buttocks, or they will expose their cleavage or breasts, or they will wear mini-skirts. These kinds of women want to be seen, and they crave attention. Young men who look at their provocative body parts and lust over them are guilty of sin. Christ said in Matthew 5:28: "**But I say to you that whoever looks at a woman to lust for her has already committed adultery with her in his heart**" (emphasis mine).

3. They are ignorant that their actions are sinful and have the potential to lead men to sin, or they do not fear the Lord's warning about causing one of God's children to sin. Christ said in Matt. 18:6: "**But whoever causes one of these little ones who believe in Me to sin, it would be better for him if a millstone were hung around his neck, and he were drowned in the depth of the sea**" (emphasis mine).

I am not trying to argue that your future wife must be legalistic. Absolutely not! Dressing a certain way cannot and will not ever save anyone. Salvation is grounded in the meritorious work of Christ alone. Nonetheless, you must be informed that young women who dress provocatively cause young men to sin (Matt. 5:28). Christ warned about the dangers that exist for those who cause God's children to sin (Matt. 18:6).

A woman who is truly regenerate will not want to do the following: cause men to sin, dishonor her husband, or offend her Lord. Therefore, if you meet a woman, and her legs and cleavage are exposed to the world, and her buttocks is flaunted for the populace to see, run from this woman. Do not consider this type of woman to be your future wife. For more instruction on the topic of modesty, examine the following passages:

> ...in like manner also, that the women adorn themselves in modest apparel, with propriety and moderation, not with braided hair or gold or pearls or costly clothing, but, **which is proper for women professing godliness**, with good works (1 Tim. 2:9-10; emphasis mine).

> **Wives, likewise, be submissive to your own husbands**, that even if some do not obey the word, they, without a word, may be won by the conduct of their wives, when they observe your chaste conduct accompanied by fear. **Do not let your adornment be merely outward—arranging the hair, wearing gold, or putting on fine apparel—rather let it be the hidden person of the heart, with the incorruptible beauty of a gentle and quiet spirit, which is very precious in the sight of God**. For in this manner, in former times, the holy women who trusted in God also adorned themselves, being submissive to their own husbands, as Sarah obeyed Abraham, calling him lord, whose daughters you are if you do good and are not afraid with any terror (1 Pet. 3:1-6; emphasis mine).

Fifth, pray for a wife who speaks in a dignified manner, not with a devilish mouth. Unconverted women who have not been discipled by their fathers or mothers will perpetually gossip, slander, joke coarsely, and use foul language. They are also contentious. The words that come out of their mouths come from their hearts. Christ said, "…For out of the abundance of the heart the mouth speaks" (Matt. 12:34).

Unconverted women will reject discipline from anyone who tells them they are wrong. Flee from these kinds of women. Read the Book of Proverbs to see why you must flee from unconverted women who do not fear the Lord:

> …And the contentions of a wife are a continual dripping (Prov. 19:13).

> Better to dwell in a corner of a housetop,
> Than in a house shared with a contentious woman
> (Prov. 21:9).

> Better to dwell in the wilderness,
> Than with a contentious and angry woman
> (Prov. 21:19).

Moreover, pray for a wife who craves the Word, not the world. A godly woman will be a wife who fears God, and proclaims the gospel to other women and her children. A godly woman will also submit to her husband's biblical guidance and authority, and will despise the things of the world.

A worldly woman will only care about temporal things such as: a nice house, a high-paying job, having lots of friends, being popular, and well liked. Therefore, it should be evident what my advice will be to you regarding a worldly woman: Pray for her salvation—and run! A wife who loves God and His Word is a wife who sets her mind on the *things above*. See Colossians 3:1-2:

If then you were raised with Christ, seek those things which are above, where Christ is, sitting at the right hand of God. Set your mind on things above, not on things on the earth.

Furthermore, pray for a wife who understands God's Word. God formed man of the dust of the ground, and breathed into his nostrils the breath of life. God then caused a deep sleep to fall on Adam. As Adam slept, God took one of his ribs, and closed up the flesh in its place. God used the rib, which He had taken from Adam and made it into a woman, and He brought her to the man. "Therefore a man shall leave his father and mother and be joined to his wife, **and they shall become one flesh**" (Gen. 2:24; emphasis mine).

In this relationship, the biblical norm for a Christian couple is "wives submit to your husbands and husbands love your wives" (Eph. 5:22-33). Husbands are to pray for their wives, make sacrifices for their wives, cherish their wives, love their wives as Christ has loved the church, and be willing to die for their wives. Most importantly, a husband's authority over his wife is grounded in the gospel of Jesus Christ.

My son, never forget: When a man leaves his mother and father, he shall be joined to his wife, "and they shall become one flesh." Women who do not submit to the Bible will despise the counsel of God regarding marriage roles and responsibilities. These complementary roles, grounded in Scripture, exist to remedy the results of the fall.

When Adam and Eve sinned against God by eating the forbidden fruit, God said to Eve: "...Your desire shall be for your husband, and he shall rule over you" (Gen. 3:16). Unregenerate women don't believe that a husband has the authority to lovingly lead in the home. This is why unconverted women will try to reverse the created order by assuming that they can rule over their husbands, which is the result of the fall. Therefore, if you meet a young woman who does not care about the authority of God's Word, you know what to do: Run!

In closing, my beloved son, you must be wise. If you are wise, you may find a wife who is beautiful—inside and out. She will fear God, and love his Word. She will believe in the true gospel. She will raise and teach godly children. She will love you. Remember, "He who finds a wife finds a good thing, and obtains favor from the LORD" (Prov. 18:22). If you fail to be wise, you will reap what you have sown. You will have to endure her continual dripping of contention. You will also need to pray that God will convert her or else you may be forced to say:

Better to dwell in a corner of a housetop,
Than in a house shared with a contentious woman
(Prov. 21:9).

I am praying for you, my son, and I love you. Be wise. Do not be unequally yoked with a woman who does not believe the true gospel. Pray that God will deliver you a godly wife who you can love and enjoy forever. Amen.

CHAPTER VIII.
MY SON, HEAR THE GOSPEL DAILY

For the gospel does not expressly demand works of our own by which we become righteous and are saved; indeed it condemns such works. Rather the gospel demands faith in Christ: that He has overcome for us sin, death, and hell, and thus gives us righteousness, life, and salvation not through our works, but through His own works, death, and suffering, in order that we may avail ourselves of His death and victory as though we have done it ourselves.

—Martin Luther

My son, if you were diagnosed with a terminal illness, you would not live your life recklessly and without the fear of death. In the same manner, you must not sleep spiritually, knowing that your mind and heart are polluted with sin. The righteousness of Christ is mighty to save. This is the good news.

Why are you a sinner? The response to this question is an essential of the gospel. Therefore, please examine the Bible to learn why you sin and the implications of it. This will help you to understand why the true gospel is good news.

At the beginning of creation, the Lord God almighty created Adam and Eve (our first parents) out of nothing and in His image. God formed Adam from the dust of the ground, and the woman from the rib of the man. God provided them with immortal souls.

The LORD God took Adam and put him in the garden of Eden to tend and keep it. And the LORD God commanded the man, saying, "Of every tree of the garden you may freely eat; but of the tree of the knowledge of good and evil you shall not eat, **for in the day that you eat of it you shall surely die**" (Gen. 2:15-17; emphasis mine).

The serpent—a manifestation of the devil—lied and deceived Eve by saying, "You will not surely die. For God knows that in the day you eat of it your eyes will be opened, and you will be like God, knowing good and evil" (Gen. 3:4-5). Instead of obeying the Lord, our first parents listened to Satan's lies. False prophets still do this today.

When Adam transgressed God's law, he represented all of mankind. As a result, the Lord placed a curse on all of mankind. Sin entered into the human race, and also death (Rom. 5:12). Put another way, Adam's sin was imputed to all men without exception. Therefore, all men are born into this world totally depraved, or desperately wicked as can be. All men are also born into this world unable and unwilling to save themselves.

The creation account explains why wicked thoughts, murder, gossip, sexual immorality, and war exist in the world today. There is a penalty to pay for committing all of these sinful acts: "**For the wages of sin is death**…" (Rom. 6:23; emphasis mine).

Therefore, how can you escape the judgment of God when you sin every day? How can God (perfectly holy and righteous) save you (sinner deserving of death) without compromising His own standard of justice? God's Word states, "He who justifies the wicked, and he who condemns the just, both of them alike are an abomination to the LORD" (Prov. 17:15). Before these questions are answered, there are several important points that you need to study.

The Bible teaches that "God is not a man, that He should lie, nor a son of man, that He should repent" (Num. 23:19). Even though you forgave someone in the past, do not think that God has to do the same. God does as He pleases (Ps. 115:3). God loves the elect, and He hates the reprobate. Therefore, do not think for a moment that God is held to your standards. See Psalm 50:21-23:

> These things you have done, and I kept silent;
> **You thought that I was altogether like you**;
> But I will rebuke you,
> And set them in order before your eyes.
> "Now consider this, you who forget God,
> Lest I tear you in pieces,
> And there be none to deliver:
> Whoever offers praise glorifies Me;
> And to him who orders his conduct aright
> I will show the salvation of God" (emphasis mine).

Study the attributes of God. God is holy, which means that His eyes are too pure to approve evil. God cannot look upon wickedness with favor (Hab. 1:13). As a result, God hates sin (Jere. 44:4), and will punish it with death (Ps. 5:4-6). This is consistent with the fact that God is righteous, which means that He is just for punishing sin with death, or whatever decision He decides to render. God is perfect.

God ordained all things, and He works all things after the counsel of His will. This means that God actively ordained the salvation of the elect, and He actively ordained the reprobation of the wicked (Rom. 9:21-23). God does as He pleases. True Christians must respond as Nebuchadnezzar did when he praised God, saying:

> For His dominion is an everlasting dominion,
> And His kingdom is from generation to generation.
> **All the inhabitants of the earth are reputed as nothing**;
> **He does according to His will in the army of heaven**
> And among the inhabitants of the earth
> **No one can restrain His hand**
> **Or say to Him, "What have You done?"**

(Dan. 4:34-35, emphasis mine)

The Bible teaches that God has provided us with types—which point to something greater—to help us understand His will. For example, going back to creation, it is easy to get lost in the scheme of things, where the serpent challenged God almighty, and our first parents lost their perfect standing and fell into sin.

In the garden, don't forget that an animal was *killed*, and it was *coats of skin* that clothed Adam and Eve in their nakedness (Gen. 3:21). What does the killing of an animal and clothes have to do with Adam and Eve's punishment in Genesis 3? This refers to Christ's substitutionary death and perfect obedience to the law, which is the whole work of Christ's righteousness in its compact unity. Christ died for the elect, and His righteousness is imputed to their accounts. Calvin said that:

> a man will be justified by faith when, excluded from the righteousness of works, he by faith lays hold of the righteousness of Christ, and clothed in it appears in the sight of God not as a sinner, but as righteous (Institutes III. xxi. 2).

According to the OT, animals were sacrificed to atone, not for the sins of everyone in the entire world, but exclusively for God's people, Israel. Pay careful attention to the text, and my exposition that will follow:

> **Speak unto the children of Israel**, saying, If a soul shall sin through ignorance against any of the commandments of the LORD concerning things which ought not to be done, and shall do against any of them: If the priest that is anointed do sin according to the sin of the people; then let him bring for his sin, which he hath sinned, **a young bullock without blemish unto the LORD for a sin offering**. And he shall bring the bullock unto the door of the tabernacle of the congregation before the LORD; **and shall lay his hand upon the bullock's**

head, and kill the bullock before the LORD. And the priest that is anointed shall take of the bullock's blood, and bring it to the tabernacle of the congregation: **And the priest shall dip his finger in the blood, and sprinkle of the blood seven times before the LORD, before the vail of the sanctuary** (Lev. 4:2-6, KJV; emphasis mine).[15]

First, you will notice that the context is Israel (God's people), and not everyone in the entire world. Yes, Israel is mentioned, but this does not mean that everyone in Israel is a child of God. Paul was very clear in the New Testament (NT) that "not all are Israel, which are of Israel" (Rom. 9:6). Paul also said that a true Jew was one who had been "circumcised in the heart" (Rom. 2:29), which is synonymous with regeneration. The term *Israel* in Leviticus 2 is a type, which signifies the elect people of God that Christ purchased with His blood.

Second, Leviticus 4 references "a young bullock without blemish." What do you think this is a type of? This signifies the Lord Jesus Christ who was without blemish, i.e., without sin (1 Pet. 1:19). The reference to a young bullock without blemish is only a type,[16] which pointed to something greater. The author of Hebrews makes it clear that the young bullock was only a type that pointed to Christ—who is holy, unstained, and separated from sinners (Heb. 7:26).

Third, consider the reasons why the priests had to "lay their hands upon the bullock's head." Scholars have referred to this as the transference of guilt. "For He made Him who knew no sin to be

---

[15] Dr. Robert Morey's work on the atonement helped me to exegete this passage. See Robert Morey, *The Saving Work of Christ: Studies in the Atonement* (Grace Abounding Ministries, 1980).

[16] The Bible teaches the following: It is impossible for the blood of bulls and goats to permanently take away sin (Heb. 10:4). The sacrifice of the animals had to be continually offered (Heb. 10:1, 11). The priests who offered sacrifices would eventually die.

sin for us, that we might become the righteousness of God in Him" (2 Cor. 5:21). This points to three imputations that you need to know: (1) Adam's sin was imputed to all men without exception. But since God loves the elect, (2) He imputed their sin to Christ, and (3) He imputes the righteousness of Christ to the elect. God is infinitely just, and He does not violate His own standard of justice. For more clarification, see Rom. 3:23-26:

> for all have sinned and fall short of the glory of God, being justified freely by His grace through the redemption that is in Christ Jesus, whom God set forth as a propitiation by His blood, through faith, to demonstrate His righteousness, because in His forbearance God had passed over the sins that were previously committed, to demonstrate at the present time His righteousness, **that He might be just and the justifier of the one who has faith in Jesus** (emphasis mine).

Fourth, the priests had to "kill the bullock before the LORD." Why did the animal have to be killed? Remember, God told Adam that "he will surely die" if he ate from the forbidden fruit. Adam and Eve sinned against God. Therefore, death is the punishment. This is why the animal (type) had to be slaughtered. The wages of sin is death! The author of Hebrews states, "And according to the law almost all things are purified with blood, **and without shedding of blood there is no remission**" (9:22; emphasis mine).

Fifth, Leviticus 4 says that the priests were required to "dip their finger in the blood, and sprinkle the blood seven times before the LORD, before the vail of the sanctuary." And according to Leviticus 17:11, "For the life of the flesh is in the blood, and I have given it to you upon the altar to make atonement for your souls; for it is the blood that makes atonement for the soul."

God is holy and righteous. Thus, the only way to enter into His presence is by appeasing Him. Those who are self-righteous think that their obedience, good works, or law-keeping can please God. This kind of self-righteousness and carnal thinking are filthy rags to God. Examine the following texts to see why good works will never save.

According to Job 15:14-16:

What is man, that he could be pure?
And he who is born of a woman, that he could be righteous?
If God puts no trust in His saints,
And the heavens are not pure in His sight,
How much less man, who is abominable and filthy,
Who drinks iniquity like water!

And according to Isaiah 64:6:

But we are all like an unclean thing,
And all our righteousnesses are like filthy rags;
We all fade as a leaf,
And our iniquities, like the wind,
Have taken us away
(emphasis mine).

The blood of Christ—sprinkled on His mercy seat—exhausted the wrath of God for the elect. This is why you must look to the work of Christ. Only the work of Christ is acceptable to God.

Christ died for the elect, not reprobate. Thus, Christ's death did not make men redeemable, reconcilable, or savable. Christ accomplished the following:

- Christ propitiated the Father's wrath for the elect.
- Christ reconciled the elect to God.
- Christ redeemed His sheep from the power of sin, death, and Satan.

- Christ redeemed His sheep from the curse of the law.
- Christ resurrected for the justification of the elect.
- Christ infallibly secured the salvation of God's elect.

The preexistent Christ is the second person of the Trinity. Christ is God, but distinct from the Father. Additionally, John 1:14 states, "And the Word became flesh and dwelt among us, and we beheld His glory, the glory as of the only begotten of the Father, full of grace and truth." The two-natured Christ is both wholly God and wholly man. Thus, Christ has two minds and two wills. This is important Christology that you need to study.

In summary, Adam transgressed the law, whereas Christ perfectly obeyed God's law. Adam sin was imputed to all men without exception. But Christ died for the elect and He resurrected for their justification. Thus, God imputed the sins of the elect to Christ, and He imputes the righteousness of Christ to the elect.

My son, you must be warned that false gospels *do* exist, and they are contrary to what you have learned thus far. Paul explained why: "But even if we, or an angel from heaven, **preach any other gospel to you than what we have preached to you**, **let him be accursed**. As we have said before, so now I say again, **if anyone preaches any other gospel to you than what you have received, let him be accursed**" (Gal. 1:8-9; emphasis mine).

Therefore, examine the differences between false teachers and God's Word:

1. False teachers: "God loves all men."
God's Word teaches that God hates the wicked (Ps. 5:4-6).

2. False teachers: "Christ died for all men."

God's Word teaches that His death was exclusively for His people (Matt. 1:21), His sheep (John 10:3, 4, 7, 11, 15, 27), those given to Him by the Father (John 6:37-40), those whom He foreknew (Rom. 8:29), and God's elect (Rom. 8:33), etc.

3. False teachers: "Accept Jesus Christ into your heart," or "walk the aisle at church."
God's Word teaches the following: Men do not choose Christ; Christ chose the elect (John 15:16); all who were appointed to eternal life believed (Acts 13:48); election is not by works, but Him who calls (Rom. 9:11); God's grace is not on the basis of works (Rom. 11:6); "not that we loved God, but that he loved us, and sent his Son to be the propitiation for our sins" (1 John 4:10), and unbelievers are born unable and unwilling to come to Christ (Rom. 3:10-18).

As unpopular as this may sound, God does not love everyone, Christ did not die for everyone, Christ's blood was not sufficient for all, and free will is a myth. God loves His elect, and He hates the wicked. Christ died for the elect, not goats. Therefore, His blood is sufficient for only the elect of God. Additionally, free will is a myth. God is faithful to save His people, and not one of His sheep will be lost, nor can anyone or anything snatch them away from Him (perseverance of the saints).

My beloved son, you must never grow tired of hearing and reading the gospel. It is not your best hope; it is your only hope. You cannot be saved by your obedience, good works, or law-keeping. Salvation is entirely of the Lord. The Father chose the elect, the Son died for the elect, and the Spirit seals the elect.

Therefore, repent and believe the gospel. Faith and repentance do not precede regeneration, nor do they merit God's favor. Faith and repentance are gifts that God gives to the elect after they have been born again. Read the gospel, hear the gospel, obey the gospel, and die for the gospel. I love you, my son.

CHAPTER IX.
MY SON, LOVE THE WORD

The Scriptures of God are my only foundation and substance in all matters of weight and importance.

—John Knox

My son, you must appeal to an ultimate standard that can define wisdom, without appealing to another standard that exists outside of it. What is an ultimate standard? An ultimate standard is the standard of standards, which is the Word of God.

The whole counsel of God is without error, and it never fails us. God's Word is true in all of its affirmations. The Bible teaches that all Scripture "is given by inspiration of God, and is profitable for doctrine, for reproof, for correction, for instruction in righteousness, that the man of God may be complete, thoroughly equipped for every good work" (2 Tim. 3:16-17).

The Word of God is sharper than any two-edged sword. Scripture is also a lamp to your feet, and a light to your path (Ps. 119:105). The world system is full of darkness and sin. Therefore, the only way to walk wisely in a world that is full of sin and darkness is to have a light to guide you.

There are several reasons why you must read and meditate on the Word of God. The Psalmist declared:

Oh, how I love Your law!
It is my meditation all the day.
You, through Your commandments, make me wiser than my enemies; For they are ever with me.
I have more understanding than all my teachers,
For Your testimonies are my meditation.
I understand more than the ancients,

Because I keep Your precepts.
I have restrained my feet from every evil way,
That I may keep Your word.
I have not departed from Your judgments,
For You Yourself have taught me.
How sweet are Your words to my taste,
Sweeter than honey to my mouth!
Through Your precepts I get understanding;
Therefore I hate every false way
(Ps. 119:97-104; emphasis mine).

Without God's Word, you will roam the earth like a blind man who constantly stumbles across things that he cannot see, unless someone helps him. You cannot walk in the dark without the light of God's Word to direct your paths. Therefore, do not be a blind man that leads other blind men. Consider the following illustration:

Taking a long road trip to a state that you never been to before will require planning. However, if you don't stop for directions, or if you fail to use a map, or if you don't use the global positioning system (GPS) on your cell phone, you will eventually get lost. This is because you decided to trust in *yourself* without seeking help to find your destination.

This is exactly what will happen if you do not seek God's Word for guidance. Listen to Christ's warning in Matt. 7:24-27:

"Therefore whoever hears these sayings of Mine, and does them, I will liken him to a wise man who built his house on the rock: and the rain descended, the floods came, and the winds blew and beat on that house; and it did not fall, for it was founded on the rock. **"But everyone who hears these sayings of Mine, and does not do them, will be like a foolish man who built his house on the sand: and the rain descended, the floods came, and the winds blew and beat on that house; and it fell. And great was its fall**" (emphasis mine).

Look to the Lord's Word. The power of God in the gospel is contained in the Word. When accompanied by the Holy Spirit, the Word of God will subdue a man, and make him a new creature. A new creature in Christ believes in the righteousness of Christ.

Do you have any idea how powerful God's Word is? God created the world and everything in it. God's Word creates life. Therefore, God ordained, controls, rules, sustains, governs, and directs all things after the counsel of His immutable will.

Read Ezekiel and you will see that the prophet was placed in the valley of dry bones. God commanded Ezekiel to proclaim His Word to the dry bones so they would live. Ezekiel 37:9 states: "Prophesy to the breath, prophesy, son of man, and say to the breath, **Thus says the Lord GOD**: Come from the four winds, O breath, and breathe on these slain, that they may live" (emphasis mine).

God's Word has the power to create life, and turn dry bones into a army. God's Word also has the power to raise the dead. Jesus cried with a loud voice, "Lazarus, come forth" (John 11:43). Lazarus was raised from the dead, and he came forth as commanded.

The Word of God is perfect, but we are not. For example, you will grow old, you will tell lies, you will have many faults, and you will never be able to say that you are perfect. You will never be able to go through life and say that you have a friend who is pure and perfect. But God's Word is perfect.

Examine Psalm 19:7-8 and you will see that the Word of God is the most perfect and pure book you could ever lay your eyes upon:

The testimony of the LORD is sure, making wise the simple;
The statutes of the LORD are right, rejoicing the heart;
The commandment of the LORD is pure, enlightening the eyes;

The wicked do not believe that the Word of God is perfect. The unregenerate will make the following comments about the Bible:

1. The Bible is just a book that was written by men.
2. The Bible is full of errors.
3. The Bible is not applicable for today.
4. The Bible is a fictional book that fundamentalists endorse.
5. The Bible is a book that misogynists use to denigrate women.
6. The Bible is a book that endorses racism and slavery.

Those who scoff and slander God's Word are not born again. Therefore, they are only doing what their unbelieving nature permits. God's Word does not contradict itself. Everything recorded in Scripture is true in all of its affirmations:

Every word of God is pure;
He is a shield to those who put their trust in Him.
Do not add to His words,
Lest He rebuke you, and you be found a liar
(Prov. 30:5-6; emphasis mine).

Scripture reveals to all of mankind that everyone has an appointed time to die. While no man can predict the date of their death, God knows the exact date and time that everyone will die. This is because God ordained all things.

My son, be grateful that God's Word stands forever, and it will never pass away:

The grass withers, the flower fades,
Because the breath of the LORD blows upon it;
Surely the people are grass.
The grass withers, the flower fades,
But the word of our God stands forever
(Is. 40:7-8; emphasis mine).

Assuredly, I say to you, this generation will by no means pass
away till all these things take place. Heaven and earth will
pass away, **but My words will by no means pass away**
(Matt. 24:34-35; emphasis mine).

You can trust in God's Word. In this life, you will have many
family and friends who will let you down. Finding reliable and
trustworthy friends and associates can be a difficult task,
depending on the profession you choose or the people you meet.
Even in the local church, you will find many professing Christians
who will not follow through on the promises they made. This can
be discouraging.

However, there is a difference between the people you meet
who struggle with being trustworthy and reliable, and God: The
people you meet are sinners, while God is sovereign. The people
you meet will make failed promises, while God fulfills all that He
pleases:

So shall My word be that goes forth from My mouth;
It shall not return to Me void,
But it shall accomplish what I please,
And it shall prosper in the thing for which I sent it
(Is. 55:11).

Can you honestly think of a day that you forgot to eat food? If
you did, I am sure that you will agree with me that it is not a
common practice. Your body will speak to you, so to speak,
through stomach pains.

As an American, you must concede that you are rich compared to all of the starving children in foreign countries. Therefore, you will be spoiled in your eating habits, which means that you will leave food on your plate, or pick off food you don't like. Starving children would give anything for your scraps.

What is my point? You do not go a day without eating, or drinking water. Your body cannot live without food and water. In the same manner, you cannot live without feeding your soul. When you neglect the Bible, you are emulating the fool who does not either. Starving yourself spiritually will leave you as a defenseless prey for Satan's attacks. Christ said that "man shall not live by bread alone, but by every word that proceeds from the mouth of God" (Matt. 4:4).

My son, I pray that you will read the Word, meditate on the Word, love the Word, and memorize the Word. The Word of God teaches that Christ perfectly obeyed the law and He died for the elect. The Word of God also teaches that the Father chose the elect, the Son died for the elect, and the Spirit seals the elect. Therefore, read the Word, son. I love you.

CHAPTER X.
MY SON, SEARCH FOR A TRUE CHURCH

Wherever we find the Word of God surely preached and heard, and the sacraments administered according to the institution of Christ, there, it is not to be doubted, is a church of God.
—John Calvin

My son, finding a true church is a difficult task, but it is important. Many so-called churches are not true churches at all. False churches are known by the fact that they do not preach the true gospel, and they embrace all of the things that God hates.

Stay far away from wicked assemblies or ministries that are associated with the following denominations: United Methodist, Roman Catholic, Episcopalian, Presbyterian Church USA, Evangelical Lutheran Church of America, United Church of Christ, Disciples of Christ, Arminian, Oneness Pentecostal, Unitarian Universalist, Church of Jesus Christ of Latter Day Saints, The Seventh-day Adventist, and Jehovah's Witnesses.

You must also be aware of the modern contemporary movement that is prevalent in America. Contemporary congregations embrace entertainment, such as rock bands, hip music leaders, movie screens, strobe lights, and watery messages from the pulpit. The gospel is not preached in these kinds of assemblies. Hireling pastors are preaching that God loves the whole world and Jesus died for everyone. They also give altar calls, so to speak, at the end of the services. This is why you need to answer the following questions: What is the church? What are the marks of a true church? Should Christians join a gospel believing church?[17]

---

[17] Joining a church is *important*, but it is *not* a condition or assurance of salvation.

To help you understand what the church is, the *Westminster Confession of Faith* (Chapter XXV, "Of the Church") provides an excellent exposition for you to study:

I. The catholic or universal Church, which is invisible, consists of the whole number of the elect, that have been, are, or shall be gathered into one, under Christ the Head thereof; and is the spouse, the body, the fullness of Him that fills all in all.

II. The visible Church, which is also catholic or universal under the Gospel (not confined to one nation, as before under the law), consists of all those throughout the world that profess the true religion; and of their children: and is the kingdom of the Lord Jesus Christ, the house and family of God, out of which there is no ordinary possibility of salvation.

III. Unto this catholic visible Church Christ has given the ministry, oracles, and ordinances of God, for the gathering and perfecting of the saints, in this life, to the end of the world: and does, by his own presence and Spirit, according to his promise, make them effectual thereunto.

IV. This catholic Church has been sometimes more, sometimes less visible. And particular Churches, which are members thereof, are more or less pure, according as the doctrine of the Gospel is taught and embraced, ordinances administered, and public worship performed more or less purely in them.

V. The purest Churches under heaven are subject both to mixture and error; and some have so degenerated, as to become no Churches of Christ, but synagogues of Satan. Nevertheless, there shall be always a Church on earth to worship God according to his will.

VI. There is no other head of the Church but the Lord Jesus Christ. Nor can the Pope of Rome, in any sense, be head thereof; but is that Antichrist, that man of sin, and son of perdition, that exalts himself, in the Church, against Christ and all that is called God.

Additionally, I will provide you with another resource to help you comprehend how a true church differs from a degenerate one—which is a bastardization of the true church. See Article 29 of the *Belgic Confession of Faith*:

We believe, that we ought diligently and circumspectly to discern from the Word of God which is the true Church, since all sects which are in the world assume to themselves the name of the Church. But we speak not here of hypocrites, who are mixed in the Church with the good, yet are not of the Church, though externally in it; but we say that the body and communion of the true Church must be distinguished from all sects, who call themselves the Church. The marks, by which the true Church is known, are these: **if the pure doctrine of the gospel is preached therein; if she maintains the pure administration of the sacraments as instituted by Christ; if church discipline is exercised in punishing of sin: in short, if all things are managed according to the pure Word of God, all things contrary thereto rejected, and Jesus Christ acknowledged as the only Head of the Church**. Hereby the true Church may certainly be known, from which no man has a right to separate himself. With respect to those, who are members of the Church, they may be known by the marks of Christians: namely, by faith; and when they have received Jesus Christ the only Savior, they avoid sin, follow after righteousness, love the true God and their neighbor, neither turn aside to the right or left, and crucify the flesh with the works thereof. But this is not to be understood, as if there did not remain in them great infirmities; but they fight against them through the Spirit, all the days of their life, continually taking their refuge in the blood, death, passion and obedience of our Lord Jesus Christ, "in whom they have remission of sins, through faith in him." As for the false Church, she ascribes more power and authority to herself and her ordinances than to the Word of God, and will not submit herself to the yoke of Christ. Neither does she administer the sacraments as appointed by Christ in his Word, but adds to and takes from them, as she thinks proper; she relieth more upon men than upon Christ; and persecutes those, who live holily according to the Word of God, and rebuke her for her errors, covetousness, and idolatry. These two Churches are easily known and distinguished from each other (emphasis mine).

Carefully review the *Belgic Confession* and how it emphasizes the marks of a true church. A true church preaches the true gospel, and exercises church discipline. Therefore, Christians who are faithful to Christ will not attend or support a congregation that does not embrace the true gospel or neglects church discipline.

A true church will have faithful preachers who will boldly proclaim the whole counsel of God, no matter how offensive it may be. A true church will also hold their members accountable. Biblically qualified elders will never allow their members to remain undisciplined if they stumble into grievous sin.

My son, when you find a true church, join it. Read Article 28 of the *Belgic Confession* to see why every believer in Christ is bound to join the local church:

We believe, since this holy congregation is an assembly of those who are saved, and that out of it there is no salvation, that no person of whatsoever state or condition he may be, ought to withdraw himself, to live in a separate state from it; but that all men are in duty bound to join and unite themselves with it; maintaining the unity of the Church; submitting themselves to the doctrine and discipline thereof; bowing their necks under the yoke of Jesus Christ; and as mutual members of the same body, serving to the edification of the brethren, according to the talents God has given them. And that this may be the more effectually observed, it is the duty of all believers, according to the word of God, to separate themselves from all those who do not belong to the Church, and to join themselves to this congregation, wheresoever God hath established it, even though the magistrates and edicts of princes were against it, yea, though they should suffer death or any other corporal punishment. Therefore all those, who separate themselves from the same, or do not join themselves to it, act contrary to the ordinance of God.

There will always be critics of local church membership. Unlettered men and women who do not study the Bible will argue that church membership is not important. I once heard a person say, "I do not need to join a local church because I can learn the Bible by myself." Sure, this person can read the Bible on their own. But if this person actually studied and understood the Bible, he would be looking for a sound church.

Additionally, biblically illiterate men and women will argue that church membership is an unbiblical tradition. This ridiculous notion must be rejected because church membership is not a tradition; it is a biblical argument that I will prove to you by addressing the following:[18]

First, church membership is biblical because Christ loved and died for His church. The Word of God states, "Husbands, love your wives, just as Christ also loved the church and gave Himself for her, that He might sanctify and cleanse her with the washing of water by the word, that He might present her to Himself a glorious church, not having spot or wrinkle or any such thing, but that she should be holy and without blemish" (Eph. 5:25-27). Christ died for His church, and He is also the head of the church (Eph. 1:22-23).

---

[18] See Mark Dever, *9 Marks of a Healthy Church* (Wheaton, IL: Crossway Books, 2004).

Second, church membership is biblical because God's Word teaches that believers must "remember the Sabbath day, to keep it holy" (Exod. 20:8). When Christ died and resurrected, the Sabbath turned into the Lord's Day—the first day of the week (1 Cor. 16:2). Therefore, since it is a commandment to observe the Sabbath Day, which is now the Lord's Day, believers are commanded to not forsake the assembly of the saints (Heb. 10:25).

Those who attend a local church will be known by their love for others (John 13:35), and they will have unity in doctrine (Eph. 4:13). According to the Bible, the manifold wisdom of God might be made known by the church to the principalities and powers in the heavenly places (Eph. 3:10).

Third, church membership is biblical because it is a foretaste of heaven. Carefully examine Revelation 21:23-27 to see why it is only the universal church or the elect who will experience heaven.

> The city had no need of the sun or of the moon to shine in it, for the glory of God illuminated it. The Lamb is its light. And the nations of those who are saved shall walk in its light, and the kings of the earth bring their glory and honor into it. Its gates shall not be shut at all by day (there shall be no night there). And they shall bring the glory and the honor of the nations into it. But there shall by no means enter it anything that defiles, or causes an abomination or a lie, **but only those who are written in the Lamb's Book of Life** (emphasis mine).

Moreover, church membership is biblical because of all of the indications and mandates that are set forth in the testimony of Scripture. Read Genesis 3:23-24, and you will see that it states: "**And the LORD God sent him out** of the garden of Eden to till the ground from which he was taken. So **He drove out the man**; and He placed cherubim at the east of the garden of Eden, and a flaming sword which turned every way, to guard the way to the tree of life" (emphasis mine). What does *sent and drove out* signify? This is a reminder that some were disciplined by being put out of the presence of God because of their rebellion.

Leviticus 13:46 and Numbers 5:3 also teach that individuals who were unclean had to dwell *outside of the camp* so they would not defile it. Being *outside* has a significant meaning. Believers in the local church have a responsibility to judge those who are inside the church, which signifies those who are members of the church. Christians are to judge righteously. Examine the Bible and you will see mandates to discipline those who are inside, i.e., members of the church.

When the church grew at Pentecost, the Bible states that, "**The Lord added to the church daily those who were being saved**" (2:47; emphasis mine). According to this verse, the Lord *adds* to the church those whom He saved, not reprobates which He will judge. The word *added* has a significant meaning: The saved are now members of the universal church.

In 1 Cor. 5:12, Paul warned about immorality and he said that it must be judged by the church. He said: "**For what have I to do with judging those also who are outside? Do you not judge those who are inside**" (emphasis mine)? The context ("inside") was referring to those who were members of the church. Paul also said, "**But those who are outside God judges. Therefore put away from yourselves the evil person**" (1 Cor. 5:13; emphasis mine).

2 Corinthians 2:6 states, "This punishment which was **by the majority** is sufficient for such a man" (emphasis mine). Christ gave the church authority to discipline (Matt. 16:19; 18:18). Therefore, only the church has the authority to discipline their

own, while God judges those on the outside, as previously stated (1 Cor. 5:13).

Read Acts 5 to learn about the story of a man named Ananias and his wife Sapphira who sold a possession, and kept back part of the proceeds. They agreed to test the Spirit of the Lord, and were subsequently killed. Therefore, great fear came upon all the church, and, "**None of the rest dared join them**…" (v. 13; emphasis mine). Those who witnessed the death of Ananias and Sapphira recognized that discipline is a serious matter. This is why they dared not *join* the church.

1 Timothy 5 teaches that Paul gave instruction to the church about honoring true widows (v. 3). This is why he said, "Do not let a widow under sixty years old **be taken into the number**…" (v. 9; emphasis mine). What does *number* mean? This is referring to their list, which had the names of all of their members.

Remember the concept of being *inside and outside*. This is important for context, especially since Paul was adamant that they were to do the following: "Refuse the younger widows; for when they have begun to grow wanton against Christ, they desire to marry, having condemnation because they have cast off their first faith. And besides they learn to be idle, wandering about from house to house, and not only idle but also gossips and busybodies, saying things which they ought not" (vv. 11-13).

Furthermore, church membership is biblical because of the authority that Christ gave the local church. Matthew 18:18 states, "Assuredly, I say to you, whatever you bind on earth will be bound in heaven, and whatever you loose on earth will be loosed in heaven." This is the authority that Christ gave the church.

Acts 6 is an important chapter about the local church. The Bible teaches that it was the local church that searched from among themselves the seven men to serve so the apostles could devote themselves to prayer and preaching (vv. 3-4). Those in the local church were pleased that they were able to choose the men (v. 5). Additionally, it was the members of the local church who laid hands on the seven men (v. 6).

Examine 1 Timothy 3:1-7 and you will see that elders are appointed to oversee the local church. Christians are to be submissive to them:

> **Obey those who rule over you, and be submissive, for they watch out for your souls, as those who must give account**. Let them do so with joy and not with grief, for that would be unprofitable for you (Heb. 13:17; emphasis mine).

My son, be wise, and find a true church. Joining a church is not a condition of salvation, nor does it mean that you have assurance of salvation. Nonetheless, finding a church is *important*.

Find a sound church where you can hear the true gospel of Christ. When you find a gospel preaching church, attend regularly and never forsake assembling with the saints (Heb. 10:25). Be a good steward and give financially to support your church (1 Cor. 16:2). Submit to the leadership who will give an account for your soul (Heb. 13:17). I love you, son.

CHAPTER XI.
MY SON, WITNESS TO THE LOST

[The godly man] is not content to go to heaven alone but wants to take others there. Spiders work only for themselves, but bees work for others. A godly man is both a diamond and a magnet – a diamond for the sparkling luster of grace and a magnet for his attractiveness. He is always drawing others to embrace piety.

–Thomas Watson

My son, being a faithful Christian means that you must tell others about the true gospel of Christ. There are many professing Christians who hear the gospel every Sunday, but don't share the good news with the lost. This is tantamount to watching an obese man gorge himself like a pig in one of the poorest countries in the world, but offers none of his food to those starving around him.

Therefore, if you claim to have been saved and given the gift of faith—yet you don't share the gospel with others—you need to determine why you are ashamed to declare Christ to the lost. Preaching to the lost is not a condition or assurance of salvation. Nonetheless, it is important. The gospel must be preached by Christians.

According to the testimony of Scripture, one of the reasons professing Christians do not witness to the lost is because they are lost themselves. Born-again believers obey the voice of their Savior who said to, "**Go into all the world and preach the gospel to every creature**" (Mark 16:15; emphasis mine), while lost individuals do not.

Think about how absurd it would be to hear a story about a firefighter who would not pick up a firehose to put out a house fire.

In the same manner, it is also absurd when professing Christians claim to believe in the good news that saves, but refuse to tell the lost about the good news that can save them.

Professing Christians who have no desire to tell the lost about Christ are sending the following message to the world:

- They are either ashamed of the gospel.
- They do not believe the gospel is mighty to save.
- They really do not care about the lost.
- They are afraid of what men will think, and not what God has commanded.
- They are not called by God to preach the gospel.

Instead of witnessing to the lost, professing Christians who do not evangelize will boldly do what they do best: They will make excuses for why they do not put their faith into practice.

There is a reason why many professing Christians do not evangelize. Their pastors don't make it a priority. Pastors who do not make evangelism a priority in their churches will inspire their members to not make evangelism a priority either.

Additionally, many pastors will argue that they have put their efforts into discipleship, but not evangelism. This is absurd. When men in the local church are discipled biblically, they will evangelize faithfully. However, since the practice of evangelism has become scarce in many churches throughout America, it is obvious that men are not being discipled by their pastors.

One of the marks of a true church is evangelism. Therefore, churches that do not practice evangelism, in my opinion, are not sound churches, but rather, social clubs.

The list of excuses never ends for pastors who do not disciple their congregations to witness to the lost. The entire Bible is a large evangelistic book. This is why many pastors are forced to come up with reasons on how they can profess to be an evangelical, but not put evangelism into practice. They are trying to soothe their Christian conscience.

Many pastors (who do not evangelize) will argue that they do not support street evangelism because there are a lot of things they see online or in person that they either do not like or fully agree with. I find it ironic how men—who do not evangelize—love to tell evangelists what they are doing wrong, or what they need to be doing right.

Many pastors will also say that they do not support evangelism because of all the *unloving and hateful* evangelists they see on the internet. These kinds of pastors fail to realize that there are also a lot of *unloving and hateful* pastors on the internet. This does not mean that every pastor should resign his position from the church because the internet is filled with *unloving and hateful* preachers. Do you know what is just as worse as the *unloving and hateful* preachers? It is the so-called pastors who are supposed to lead their churches to witness to the world, but are silent and do not evangelize at all!

Pastors must be encouraged to make evangelism a priority in their local churches. Pastors fall into a dangerous trap when they tell others to do something that they themselves do not do. Pastors are commanded to teach the Bible. Thus, it is impossible for any faithful preacher of the Word to avoid preaching on evangelism.

How can a pastor tell his congregation to evangelize the lost if he does not witness to the lost? This is not heroism—it is hypocrisy. In Matthew 23, Christ warned about certain men, hypocritical Pharisees, who told others to do things that they themselves would not do.

The so-called shepherds who have ignored the practice of evangelism will tell their congregants to do the work of the evangelist, while they do not evangelize at all. Therefore, many of their members will repeat these same practices. This is why many professing Christians have abandoned the practice of evangelism for excuses. This chapter will address a few.

Sadly, cults (i.e., Mormons, etc.) are out in their communities exercising their pagan faith, while many professing Christians are silent, or they will make excuses. Don't be surprised when you hear professing conservative Christians say that they are adamantly against abortion, yet they won't evangelize at abortions clinics. Roman Catholics are the ones who are at the abortion clinics, while most so-called conservative Christians won't go at all.

When you hear a person say, "I am a Christian, but I am not called to evangelize," remind this person that their argument is tantamount to listening to a firefighter tell his co-workers, "I am a firefighter, but I am not called to put out fires." Any reasonable and logical person would want to know why the firefighter is in the profession of firefighting if he is not called to put out fires. In the same manner, any reasonable and logical person would also want to know why a Christian is in the profession of Christianity if they will not tell the lost about Christ.

I don't have time to evangelize is another excuse that is not uncommon. Men who make this kind of excuse need to be asked this important question: "If you can make time for movies, sports games, watching television sitcoms, hanging out with friends, or serving on boards or committees, but will not make time to evangelize as God has commanded, why can't you make time to tell the lost about the true gospel? I am not arguing that men must neglect their families in order to make time for evangelism. Absolutely not! Christians should make time for evangelism if they can make time for everything else.

My son, instead of making excuses, you must evangelize. When you evangelize, you will be scoffed at, despised by many, and possibly assaulted because of the gospel that you believe and preach. Are you willing to suffer for Christ?

Please remember that homosexuals, Roman Catholics, Muslims, Jehovah's Witnesses, and professing atheists will not attend your local church. They hate the gospel. This is why you need to take the gospel to the lost.

In closing, you must witness to the lost. It is easy to get discouraged. Nonetheless, you must be faithful. You will meet professing Christians who will say that they love the lost, but will not witness to them. Do not be like them.

My beloved son, if you suffer for Christ, count it worthy to do so for Christ's sake. In Acts 5:41, the apostles "departed from the presence of the council, **rejoicing that they were counted worthy to suffer shame for his name**" (emphasis mine).

Remain wise, speak the truth in love, and stay bold. I love you, my son. Remember the words of our Savior:

When He had called the people to Himself, with His disciples also, He said to them, "**Whoever desires to come after Me, let him deny himself, and take up his cross, and follow Me.** For whoever desires to save his life will lose it, but whoever loses his life for My sake and the gospel's will save it. For what will it profit a man if he gains the whole world, and loses his own soul? Or what will a man give in exchange for his soul? **For whoever is ashamed of Me and My words in this adulterous and sinful generation, of him the Son of Man also will be ashamed when He comes in the glory of His Father with the holy angels**" (Mark 8:34-38; emphasis mine).

CONCLUSION

My son, do not forget my law,
But let your heart keep my commands;
For length of days and long life
And peace they will add to you.
Let not mercy and truth forsake you;
Bind them around your neck,
Write them on the tablet of your heart,
And so find favor and high esteem
In the sight of God and man.
Trust in the Lord with all your heart,
And lean not on your own understanding;
In all your ways acknowledge Him,
And He shall direct your paths.
Do not be wise in your own eyes;
Fear the Lord and depart from evil.
It will be health to your flesh,
And strength to your bones
(Prov. 3:1-8).

My son, after reading this devotional work, you will see why devoting yourself to reading Scripture every day is important. The world we live in is wicked, and you are a sinner. Nothing good ever happens when a wicked sinner becomes a friend with this wicked world. Therefore, do not follow the path of those who have made themselves an enemy of God (Jam. 4:4).

You must establish preventive measures to protect yourself from all of the bait that Satan has planted in the world. You will encounter many things in this life. This is why you must avoid falling into these traps that have the potential to harm you.

You need to rely on the wisdom of God's Word. The Word of God explains the true gospel of Jesus Christ, and it provides lots of instruction for you to follow. This will help you to carefully think about your actions before you say or do something that will dishonor God.

You must never put yourself in a predicament that you will regret. Never forget: "...**be sure your sin will find you out**" (Num. 32:23; emphasis mine). Therefore, stay away from night clubs, late night parties, social events that promote immorality, and from worldly women and friends.

Read the Book of Proverbs daily to gain invaluable insight on how you are to conduct yourself. Do not wake up in the morning and think for one moment that you can go a day without being instructed on how to be wise. The Bible says, "**He who trusts in his own heart is a fool, but whoever walks wisely will be delivered**" (Prov. 28:26; emphasis mine).

In the appendix, I have provided you with an invaluable resource that I pray you will cherish: *John Calvin's Catechism*. This *Catechism* is doctrinally sound, and it is a form of instruction for children. Therefore, study the Book of Proverbs to be wise, and catechize your mind with the purity of Scripture.

Remember, your obedience to Christ, good works, law-keeping, or abstaining from worldly things are not conditions or assurance of salvation. Christ is the only grounds of justification, and assurance of salvation.

My son, give me your *heart* (undivided attention). I love you.

APPENDIX
JOHN CALVIN'S CATECHISM[19]

I. OF FAITH

1. Minister. What is the chief end of human life?
Child. To know God.

2. Why do you say that?
Because He created us and placed us in this world to be glorified in us.
And it is indeed right that our life, of which He Himself is the beginning,
should be devoted to His glory.

3. What is the sovereign good of man?
The same thing.

4. Why do you hold that to be the sovereign good?
Because without it our condition is more miserable than that of brute-
beasts.

**5. Hence, then, we see that nothing worse can happen to a man than
to live without God.**
It is so.

6. What is the true and right knowledge of God?
When we know Him in order that we may honour Him.

7. How do we honour Him aright?
We put our reliance on Him, by serving Him in obedience to His will, by
calling upon Him in all our need, seeking salvation and every good thing
in Him, and acknowledging with heart and mouth that all our good
proceeds from Him.

**8. To consider these things in order, and explain them more fully——
–what is the first point?**
To rely upon God.

---

[19] "Calvin's Catechism - by Dr. John Calvin." *A Puritan's Mind*,
www.apuritansmind.com/creeds-and-confessions/calvins-catechism-by-dr-john-
calvin/. Retrieved on December 10, 2018.

9. How can we do that?
First by knowing Him as almighty and perfectly good.

10. Is this enough?
No.

11. Why?
Because we are unworthy that He should show His power in helping us, or employ His goodness toward us.

12. What more then is required?
That we be certain that He loves us, and desires to be our Father, and Saviour.

13. How do we know that?
By His Word, in which He declares His mercy to us in Christ, and assures us of His love toward us.

14. Then the foundation for true reliance upon God is to know Him in Jesus Christ [John 17:3]?
That is true.

15. What then briefly is the substance of this knowledge?
It is contained in the Confession of Faith used by all Christians. It is commonly called the Apostles' Creed, because it is a summary of the true faith which has always been held in Christ's Church, and was derived from the pure doctrine of the Apostles.

16. Recite it.

17. In order to expound this confession in detail, into how many parts do we divide it?
Into four principal parts.

18. What are they?
The first is about God the Father; the second about His Son Jesus Christ, which also includes the whole history of our redemption; the third is about the Holy Spirit; the fourth is about the Church, and the gracious gifts of God conferred on her.

19. Since there is but one God, why do you mention the Father, Son, and Holy Spirit, who are three?

Because in the one essence of God, we have to look on the Father as the beginning and origin, and the first cause of all things; then the Son, who is Eternal Wisdom; and the Holy Spirit who is His virtue and power shed abroad over all creatures, but still perpetually resident in Himself.

20. You mean then that there is no objection to our understanding that these three persons are distinctly in one Godhead, that therefore God in not therefore divided?
Just so.

21. Now repeat the first part.
"I believe in God the Father Almighty, Maker of heaven and earth."

22. Why do you call Him Father?
It is with reference to Christ who is His eternal Word, begotten of Him before time, and being sent into this world was demonstrated and declared to be His Son. But since God is the Father of Jesus Christ, it follows that He is our Father also.

23. In what sense do you mean that He is Almighty?
That does not mean that He has a power which He does not exercise, but that He disposes all things by His Providence, governs the world by His will, ruling all as it seems good to Him.

24. You mean that the power of God is not idle, but consider rather that His hand is always engaged in working, so that nothing is done except through Him, with His permission and His decree.
It is so.

25. Why do you add that He is Creator of heaven and earth?
Because He has manifested Himself to us by works [Ps. 104; Rom. 1:20] we ought to seek Him in them. Our mind cannot comprehend His essence. But the world is for us like a mirror in which we may contemplate Him in so far as it is expedient for us to know Him.

26. Do you not understand by "heaven and earth" all other creatures?
Yes, indeed; under these two words all are included, because they are all heavenly and earthly.

27. But why do you call God a Creator only, seeing that it is much more to uphold and preserve creatures in their state, than to have

once created them?

This term does not signify that God brought His works into being at a single stroke, and then left them without a care for them. We ought rather to understand, that as the world was made by God in the beginning, so now it is preserved by Him in its estate, so that the heavens, the earth and all creatures do no continue in their being apart from this power. Besides, seeing that He holds all things in His hand, it follows that the government and lordship over them belongs to Him. Therefore, in that He is Creator of heaven and earth, it is His to rule the whole order of nature by His goodness and power and wisdom. It is He who sends rain and drought, hail, tempest and fair weather, fruitfulness and barrenness, health and sickness. In short, all things are under His command, to serve Him as it seems good to Him.

28. But what about wicked men and devils? Are they also subject to Him?

Although He does not guide them by His Holy Spirit, nevertheless He curbs them by His power, so that they cannot budge unless He permits them. He even constrains them to execute His will, although it is against their own intention and purpose.

29. What good do you derive from the knowledge of this fact?

Very much. It would go ill with us if devils and wicked men had power to do anything in spite of the will of God. Moreover, we could never be at rest in our minds if we were exposed to them in danger, but when we know that they are curbed by the will of God, so that they can do nothing without His permission, then we may rest and breathe again, for God has promised to protect and defend us.

30. Let us now come to the second part.

"And in Jesus Christ His only Son our Lord", etc.

31. What briefly does it comprehend?

That we acknowledge the Son of God as our Saviour, and the means by which He has redeemed us from death, and acquired salvation.

32. What is the meaning of the name Jesus which you give to Him?

It means Saviour, and was given to Him by the angel at the command of God (Matt. 1:21).

33. Is this of more importance than if men had given it?

Oh, yes. For since God wills that He be called so, He must be so in truth.

34. What, next, is meant by the name of Christ?

By this title His office is still better expressed—for it signifies that He was appointed by the Father to be ordained King, Priest, and Prophet.

35. How do you know that?

Because according to the Scripture, anointing is used for these three things. Also, because they are attributed to Him many times.

36. But with what kind of oil was He anointed?

Not with visible oil as was used for ancient kings, priests, and prophets, but this anointing was by the grace of the Holy Spirit, who is the reality signified by that outward anointing made in time past (Isa. 61:1, Ps. 45:7).

37. But what is this Kingdom of which you speak?

It is spiritual, and consists in the Word and Spirit of God, and includes righteousness and life.

38. What of the priesthood?

It is the office and prerogative of presenting Himself before God to obtain grace and favour, and appease His wrath in offering a sacrifice which is acceptable to Him.

39. In what sense do you call Christ a Prophet?

Because on coming down into the world (Isa. 7:14) He was the sovereign messenger and ambassador of God His Father, to give full exposition of God's will toward the world and so put an end to all prophecies and revelations (Heb. 1:2).

40. But do you derive any benefit from this?

All this is for our good. For Jesus Christ has received all these gifts in order that He may communicate them to us, and that all of us may receive out of His fullness.

41. Expound this to me more fully.

He received the Holy Spirit in full perfection with all His graces, that He may lavish them upon us and distribute them, each according to the measure and portion which the Father knows to be expedient (Eph. 4:7). Thus, we may draw from Him as from a fountain all the spiritual blessings we possess.

42. What does His Kingdom minister to us?

By it, we are set at liberty in our conscience and are filled with His spiritual riches in order to live in righteousness and holiness, and we are also armed with power to overcome the Devil, the flesh, and the world——the enemies of our souls.

43. What about His priesthood?

First, by means of it He is the Mediator who reconciles us to God His Father; and secondly, through Him we have access to present ourselves to God, and offer Him ourselves in sacrifice with all that belongs to us. And in this way we are companions of His priesthood.

44. There remains His Prophetic Office.

Since this office was given to the Lord Jesus to be the Master and Teacher of His own, its end is to bring us the true knowledge of the Father and of His Truth, so that we may be scholars in the household of God.

45. You would conclude, then, that the title of Christ includes three offices which God has given His Son, in order to communicate virtue and fruit to His faithful people?

That is so.

46. Why do you call Him the only Son of God, seeing that God calls us all His children?

We are children of God not by nature, but only by adoption and by grace, in that God wills to regard us as such (Eph. 1:5). But the Lord Jesus who was begotten of the substance of His Father, and is of one essence with Him, is rightly called the only Son of God (John 1:14; Heb. 1:2) for there is no other who is God's Son by nature.

47. You mean to say, then, that this honour is proper to Him alone, and belongs to Him by nature, but is communicated to us through a gracious gift, in that we are His numbers.

That is so. Hence, in regard to this communication He is called elsewhere "the First-born among many brethren" (Rom. 8:29; Col. 1:15).

48. How is He "our Lord"?

Because He is appointed by the Father to have us under His government, to administer the Kingdom and the Lordship of God in heaven and on earth, and to be the Head of men and believers (Eph. 5:23; Col. 1:18).

49. What is meant by what follows?
It declares how the Son of God was anointed by the Father to be our Saviour. That is to say, He assumed human flesh, and accomplished all things necessary to our salvation, as enunciated here.

50. What do you mean by the two clauses, "Conceived of the Holy Ghost, born of the Virgin Mary"?
That He was formed in womb of the Virgin Mary, of her proper substance, to be the seed of David, as had been foretold (Ps. 132:11), and yet that this was wrought by the miraculous operation of the Holy Spirit, without the cooperation of a man (Matt. 1:18; Luke 1:35).

51. Was it then required that He should put on our very flesh?
Yes, because it was necessary that the disobedience committed by man against God should be redressed in human nature. And moreover He could not otherwise be our Mediator to reconcile us to God His Father (1 Tim. 2:5; Heb. 4:15).

52. You say that Christ had to become man, to fulfill the office of Saviour, as in our very person.
Yes, indeed. For we must recover in Him all that we lack in ourselves, and this cannot be done in any other way.

53. But why was that effected by the Holy Spirit, and not by the work of man according to the order of nature?
As the seed of man is in itself corrupt, it was necessary that the power of the Holy Spirit should intervene in this conception, in order to preserve our Lord from all corruption, and to fill Him with holiness.

54. Thus we are shown that He who is to sanctify others was free from every stain, and from His mother's womb He was consecrated to God in purity from the very beginning, in order that He may not be subject to the universal corruption of the human race.
So I understand it.

55. Why do you go immediately from His birth to His death, passing over the whole history of His life?
Because nothing is said here about what belongs properly to the substance of our redemption.

56. Why is it not said simply and in a word that He died while Pontius Pilate is spike of, under whom He suffered?

That is not only to make us certain of the history, but is also meant to signify that His death involved condemnation.

57. How is that?
He died to suffer the punishment due to us, and thus to deliver us from it. However, because we were guilty before the judgment of God as evil-doers, in order to represent us in person He was pleased to appear before the tribunal of an earthly judge, and to be condemned by his mouth, that we might be acquitted before the throne of the celestial Judge.

58. But Pilate pronounced Him innocent, and therefore did not condemn Him as if He were worthy of death (Matt. 27:24; Luke 23:14).
Both were involved. He was justified by the testimony of the judge, to show that He did not suffer for His own unworthiness but for ours and yet He was solemnly condemned by the sentence of the same judge, to show that He is truly our surety, receiving condemnation for us in order to acquit us from it.

59. That is well said, for if He had been a sinner He could not have suffered death for others; and yet in order that His condemnation might be our deliverance, He had to be reckoned among transgressors (Is. 53:12).
I understand so.

60. Is there greater importance in His having been crucified than if He had been put death in another way?
Yes, as Paul also shows us when he says that He hanged on a tree to take our curse upon Himself and acquit us of it (Gal. 3:13). For that kind of death was accursed of God (Deut. 21:23).

61. What? Is it not to dishonour the Lord Jesus, to say He was subjected to the curse, and that before God?
By no means, for in taking it upon Himself He abolished it, by His power, yet in such a way that He did not cease to be blessed throughout in order that He might fill us with His blessing.

62. Explain the rest.
Since death was the curse on man as a result of sin, Jesus Christ has endured it, and in enduring it overcame it. And to show that He underwent a real death, He chose to be placed in the tomb like other men.

63. But nothing seems to redound to us from this victory, since we do not cease to die.

That is no obstacle. The death of believers is nothing else than a way of entering into a better life.

64. Hence, it follows that we ought no longer to dread death as if it were a fearful thing, but we should willingly follow Jesus Christ our Head and Captain, who precedes us, not in order to let us perish, but in order to save us.

That is so.

65. What is the meaning of the additional clause: "He descended into hell"?

That He not only suffered natural death, which is the separation of the body from the soul, but also that His soul was pierced with amazing anguish, which St. Peter calls the pains of death (Acts 2:24).

66. Why and how did that happen to Him?

Because He presented Himself to God in order to make satisfaction in the name of sinners, it was necessary that He should suffer fearful distress of conscience, as if He had been forsaken by God, and even as if God had become hostile to Him. It was in this extremity that He cried, "My God, my God, why hast thou forsaken me?" (Matt. 27:46; Mark 15:34).

67. Was His Father then opposed to Him?

No. But He had to be afflicted in this way in fulfillment of what had been foretold by Isaiah, that "he was smitten by the hand of God for our sins and wounded for our transgressions" (Is. 53:5; 1 Pet. 2:24).

68. But since He is God Himself, how could He be in such dread, as if He were forsaken by God?

We must hold that it was according to His human nature that He was in that extremity: and that in order to allow this, His Deity held itself back a little, as if concealed, that is, did not how its power.

69. How is it possible that Jesus Christ, who is the salvation of the world, should have been under such damnation?

He was not to remain under it. For though He experienced the horror we have spoken of, He was by no means oppressed by it. On the contrary, He battled with the power of hell, to break and destroy it.

70. Thus we see the difference between the torment which He suffered and that which sinners experience when God punishes them in His wrath. For what He suffered for a time in Himself is perpetual in the others, and what was only a needle to sting Him is to them a sword to deliver a mortal wound.

It is so, for Jesus Christ, even in the midst of such distress, did not cease to hope in God. But sinners whom God condemns rush into despair, defy, and even blaspheme Him.

71. May we not gather from this what fruit we receive from the death of Jesus Christ?

Yes, indeed. And, first, we see that it is a sacrifice by which He has made satisfaction for us before the judgment of God, and so has appeased the wrath of God and reconciled us to Him. Secondly, that His blood is the laver by which our souls are cleansed from all stains. Finally, that by this death our sins are effaced, so as never to be remembered before God, and thus the debt which was against us is abolished.

72. Do we not have any other benefit from it?

Yes, we do. If we are true members of Christ, our old man is crucified, our flesh is mortified, so that evil desires no longer reign in us.

73. Expound the next article.

This is: "On the third day He rose again from the dead." By this He declared Himself the conqueror of death and sin, for by His resurrection He swallowed up death, broke the fetters of the devil, and destroyed all his powers (1 Pet. 3:22).

74. In how many ways does this resurrection benefit us?

First, by it righteousness was fully acquired for us. Secondly, it is also a sure pledge to us that we shall rise again one day in immortal glory (1 Cor. 15:20-23). Thirdly, if we truly participate in His resurrection, even now we are raised in newness of life, to serve God and to live a holy life according to His pleasure (Rom. 6:4).

75. Continue.

"He ascended into heaven."

76. Did He ascend in such a way that He is no longer on earth?

Yes. For after He had performed all that He was enjoined by the Father, and was required for our salvation, there was no need for Him to remain on earth.

77. What benefit do we obtain from this ascension?

The benefit is twofold. For inasmuch as Jesus Christ entered heaven in our name, as He had descended for our sake, He has given us an entry, and assured us that the door, previously shut because of sin, is now open for us (Rom. 6:8-11). Secondly, He appears before the face of the Father as our Intercessor and Advocate (Heb. 7:25).

78. But did Christ in going to heaven withdraw from us, in such a way that He has now ceased to be with us?

No. On the contrary, He has promised that He will be with us to the end (Matt. 28:20).

79. Is it in bodily presence that He remains with us?

No, for it is one thing to speak of His body which was taken up into heaven, and another to speak of His power, which is spread abroad everywhere (Luke 24:51; Acts 2:33).

80. How do you understand that He "sitteth on the right hand of the Father?

It means that He has received the dominion of heaven and earth, so that He reigns and rules over all (Matt. 28:18).

81. But what is meant by "right hand," and by "sitteth"?

It is a similitude taken from earthly princes, who are wont to place on their right hand those whom they make their lieutenants to govern in their name.

82. You do not mean anything more then than Paul when he says that Christ had been appointed Head of the Church, and raised above all principality, has secured a Name which is above every name (Eph. 1:22; 4:15; Phil. 2:9).

That is so.

83. Continue.

"From thence He will come to judge the quick and the dead." That is to say, He will appear again from heaven in judgment, as He was seen to ascend (Acts 1:11).

84. As the judgment is not to be before the end of the world, how do you say that some men will then be alive, and thus will be dead,

seeing it is appointed to al men once to die? (Heb. 9:27, 28).
Paul answers this question when he says, that those who then survive
will suddenly be changed so that their corruption will be abolished, and
their bodies will put on incorruption (1 Cor. 15:52; 1 Thess. 4:17).

**85. You understand then that this change will be for them like a
death, for it will abolish their first nature, and raise them up in a
new state.**
That is it.

**86. Does the fact that Christ is to come gain to judge the world bring
us any consolation?**
Yes, indeed. For we are certain that He will appear only for our
salvation.

**87. We should not then fear the last judgment, and have a horror of
it?**
No, since we are not to come before any other judge then He who is our
Advocate, and who has taken our cause in hand to defend us.

88. Let us come now to the third part.
This is faith in the Holy Spirit.

89. What do we gain by it?
The knowledge that as God has redeemed and saved us by Jesus Christ,
He will also make us partakers of this redemption and salvation, through
His Holy Spirit.

90. How?
As the blood of Christ is our cleansing, the Holy Spirit must sprinkle our
consciences with it that they may be cleansed (1 Pet. 1:19).

91. This requires a clearer explanation.
I mean that the Holy Spirit, while He dwells in our hearts, makes us feel
the virtue of our Lord Jesus (Rom. 5:5). For He enlightens us to know
His benefits; He seals and imprints them in our souls, and makes room
for them in us (Eph. 1:13). He regenerates us and makes us new
creatures, so that through Him we receive all the blessings and gifts
which are offered to us in Jesus Christ.

92. What follows?
The fourth part, where it is said that we believe in the Catholic Church.

93. What is the Catholic Church?
The community of the faithful which God has ordained and elected to eternal life.

94. Is it necessary to believe this article?
Yes, indeed, unless we want to make the death of Christ of none effect, and all that has already been said. The fruit that proceeds from it is the Church.

95. You mean then that up to this point we have spoken of the cause and foundation of salvation, how God has received us in love through the mediation of Jesus, and has confirmed this grace in us through His Holy Spirit. But now the effect and fulfillment of all this is explained in order to give us greater certainty.
It is so.

96. In what sense do you call the Church holy?
All whom God has chosen He justifies, and reforms to holiness and innocence, that His glory may be reflected in them (Rom. 8:30). And so Jesus Christ sanctified the Church which He redeemed, that it might be glorious and without blemish (Eph. 5:25-27).

97. What is meant by the word Catholic or Universal?
It is meant to signify, that there is only one Head of the faithful, so they must all be united in one body, so that there are not several churches but one only, which is extended throughout the whole world (Eph. 4:15; 1 Cor. 12:12 and 27).

98. And what is the meaning of what follows concerning the communion of saints?
That is added to express more clearly the unity which exists among the members of the Church. Moreover by this we are given to understand, that all the benefits that the Lord gives to the Church, are for the good and salvation of every Church, because they all have communion together.

99. But is this holiness which you attribute to the Church already perfect?
Not as long as she battles in this world, for elements of imperfection

always remain and will never be entirely removed, until she is united completely to Jesus Christ her Head, by whom she is sanctified.

100. Can this Church be known in any other way than by believing in her?

There is indeed the visible Church of God, for the recognition of which He has certain signs, but here we speak properly of the fellowship of those whom He has elected to salvation which cannot be seen plainly by the eye.

101. What comes next?

I believe in "the forgiveness of sins".

102. What do you understand by this word "forgiveness"?

That God by His pure goodness forgives and pardons the sins of believers, so that they are not brought to account before His judgment, in order to be punished.

103. Hence it follows that it is not at all through our own satisfaction that we desire to have God's pardon?

That is true; for the Lord Jesus has made payment and born the punishment. We on our part could not make any recompense to God, but may only receive pardon for all our misdeeds through the pure generosity of God.

104. Why do you insert this article after the Church?

Because no man obtains pardon for his sins without being previously incorporated into the people of God, persevering in unity and communion with the Body of Christ in such a way as to be a true member of the Church.

105. And so outside the Church there is nothing but damnation and death?

Certainly, for all those who separate themselves from the community of the faithful to form a sect on its own, have no hope of salvation so long as they are in schism.

106. What follows?

I believe in "the resurrection of the flesh and the life everlasting".

107. Why is this article inserted?

To show us that our happiness is not situated on the earth. This serves a two-fold end. We are to learn to pass through this world as though it were a foreign country, treating lightly all earthly things and declining to set our hearts on them. Secondly, we are not to lose courage, no matter how much we fail to perceive as yet the fruit of the grace which the Lord has wrought for us in Jesus Christ, but wait patiently until the time of revelation.

108. How will this resurrection take place?
Those who were formerly dead will resume their bodies, but with another quality; that is, they will no longer be subject to death or corruption, even although their substance will remain the same. Those who will survive God will miraculously raise up through a sudden change, as it is said (1 Cor. 15:52).

109. Will this resurrection not be common to the evil and the good?
Yes indeed, but not in the same way. Some will rise to salvation and joy, others to condemnation and death (John 5:29; Matt. 25:46).

110. Why then is eternal life only spoken of here, and hell not at all?
Because nothing is set down in this summary that does not tend to the consolation of faithful consciences. It relates to us only the benefits which God performs for His servants. Accordingly no mention is made of the wicked, who are excluded from His Kingdom.

111. Since we have the foundation on which faith is laid, we should be quite able to gather from it what true faith is.
Yes, indeed, It is a sure and steadfast knowledge of the love of God toward us, according as He declares in His gospel that He is our Father and Saviour (through the mediation of Jesus Christ).

112. Can we have this by ourselves, or does it come from God?
Scripture teaches that it is the singular gift of the Holy Spirit, and experience also demonstrates it.

113. How so?
Our mind is too weak to comprehend the spiritual wisdom of God which is revealed to us by faith, and our hearts are too prone either to defiance or to a perverse confidence in ourselves or creaturely things. But the Holy Spirit enlightens us to make us capable of understanding what would otherwise be incomprehensible to us, and fortifies us in certitude, sealing and imprinting the promises of salvation on our hearts.

114. What good comes to us from this faith, when we have it?

It justifies us before God, and makes us obtain eternal life.

115. How so? Is not man justified by good works in a holy life and in conformity to God?

If any one be found so perfect, he might well be deemed righteous, but since we are all poor sinners, we must look elsewhere for a worthiness in which to make answer before the judgment of God.

116. But are all our works so reprobate that they cannot merit grace before God?

First, all that we do of ourselves, by our own nature, is vicious, and therefore cannot please God. He condemns them all.

117. You say then that before God has received us in His grace, we can nothing but sin, just as a bad tree cannot but produce bad fruit? (Matt. 7:17).

It is so. For even if our works appear beautiful outwardly, yet they are evil, since the heart, to which God looks, is perverted.

118. Hence you conclude, that we cannot by our merits anticipate God, and so induce Him to be kind to us, but on the contrary that we do nothing but provoke Him to be against us?

Yes. And therefore I say: merely through His goodness, without any regard to our works, He is pleased to accept us freely in Jesus Christ, imputing His righteousness to us, and does not impute our sins to us (Tit. 3:5-7).

119. What do you mean then by saying that a man is justified by faith?

That in believing the promises of the gospel and in receiving them in true affiance of the heart, we enter into this righteousness.

120. You mean then that as God offers righteousness to us by the gospel, so it is by faith that we receive it?

Yes.

121. But after God has once received us, are the works which we do by His grace, not pleasing to Him?

Yes, they are, in that He generously accepts them, not however in virtue of their own worthiness.

122. How is that? Are they not accepted as worthy, seeing that they proceed from the Holy Spirit?
No. For there is always some weakness in them, the weakness of our flesh, through which they are defiled.

123. By what means, then, are they made acceptable?
It is by faith. That is to say, that a person is assured in his conscience that God will not examine him harshly, but covering his defects and impurities by the purity of Jesus Christ, He will regard him as perfect.

124. But can we say from this that a Christian man is justified by works after God has called him, or that through them he merits the love of God, and so obtains eternal life?
No. On the contrary, it is said that no man living will be justified in His sight (Ps. 143:2). Therefore we have to pray that He will not enter into judgment with us, nor call us to account.

125. You do not mean therefore that the good works of believers are useless?
No. For God promises to reward them fully, both in this world and in Paradise. But this comes from His gratuitous love toward us: moreover He buries all our faults, so as never to remember them.

126. But can we believe that we are justified, without doing good works?
That is impossible. For to believe in Jesus Christ is to receive Him as He has given Himself to us. He promises not only to deliver us from death and restore us to favour with God His Father, through the merit of His innocence, but also to regenerate us by His Spirit, that we may be enabled to live in holiness.

127. Faith, then, not only does not make us careless of good works, but is the root from which they are produced.
It is so, and for this reason, the doctrine of the Gospel is comprehended in these two points, faith and repentance.

128. What is repentance?
Dissatisfaction with and a hatred of evil and a love good proceeding from the fear of God, and inducing us to mortify our flesh, so that we may be governed and led by the Holy Spirit, in the service of God.

129. But this second point we have mentioned concerning the Christian life.
Yes, and we said that the true and legitimate service of God is to obey His will.

130. Why?
Because He will not be served according to our own imagination, but in the way that pleases Him.

II. OF LAW, THAT IS THE TEN COMMANDMENTS OF GOD

131. What rule has He given us by which we may direct our life?
His law.

132. What does it contain?
It is divided into two parts: the first contains four commandments, the other six. Thus there are ten in all.

133. Who made this division?
God Himself, who delivered it to Moses written on two table, and declared that it was reduced into ten words. (Exod. 32:15; 34:29; Deut. 4:13; 10:1).

134. What is the content of the first table?
The Way of the true worship of God.

135. And the second?
How we are to live with our neighbours, and what we owe them.

136. Repeat the first commandment.
Hear, O Israel, I am the Lord thy God, who brought thee out of the land of Egypt, out of the house of bondage: thou shalt have no other gods before Me (Exod. 20:2-3; Deut. 5:6-7).

137. Explain the meaning.
At first He makes a kind of preface for the whole law. For in calling Himself the Eternal and the Creator of the world, He claims authority to command. Then He declares that He is our God, in order that we may esteem His doctrine. For if He is our Saviour, that is good reason why we should be an obedient people to Him.

138. But is not that which He says after the deliverance from the land of Egypt, addressed particularly to the people of Israel?
Yes, it does refer to the physical deliverance of Israel, but it also applies to us all in a general way, in that He has delivered our souls from the spiritual captivity of sin, and the tyranny of the devil.

139. Why does He mention this at the beginning of His law?
To remind us how much we are bound to obey His good pleasure, and what gratitude it should be on our part if we do the contrary.

140. And what does He require briefly in this first commandment?
That we reserve for Him alone the honour that belongs to Him, and do not transfer it elsewhere.

141. What is the honour due Him?
To adore Him alone, to call upon Him, to have our affiance in Him, and all similar things due to His majesty.

142. Why is it said "Before my face"?
Since He who sees and knows all is the judge of the secret thoughts of men, it means that He wants to be worshiped as God, not only by outward confession, but also in pure trust and affection of heart.

143. Turn to the second Commandment.
Thou shalt not make unto thee a graven image, nor any form that is in heaven above, or on the earth beneath, or in the water under the earth. Thou shalt not do honour to them.

144. Does He entirely forbid us to make any image?
No, but He forbids us to make any image with which to represent God, or to worship Him.

145. Why is it unlawful to represent God visibly?
Because there is no resemblance between Him who is eternal Spirit and incomprehensible, and corporal, dead, corruptible and visible matter (Deut. 4:15; Isa. 40:7; Rom. 1:23; Acts 17:24-25).

146. You think then that it does dishonour to His majesty to represent Him in this way?
Yes.

147. What kind of worship is here condemned?

When we come before an image intending to pray, or bow our knee before it; or to make any other sign of reverence, as if God were there showing Himself to us.

148. This does not mean that all sculpture or painting is universally forbidden, but only all images used in the service of God, or in worshiping Him in visible things, or indeed for any abuse of them in idolatry of any kind whatsoever.

That is so.

149. Now to what end shall we refer this commandment?

With the first commandment, God declared that He alone, and no one beside Him, should be worshiped: so now He shows us the correct form of worship, in order that He may draw us away from all superstitions, and carnal ceremonies.

150. Let us proceed.

He adds a warning that He is the Eternal, our God, strong and jealous, visiting the iniquity of the fathers upon the children of them who hate Him, to the third and fourth generation.

151. Why does He make mention of His might?

To indicate that He has power to maintain His glory.

152. What is meant by jealousy?

That He cannot allow an associate. For as He has given Himself to us out of His infinite goodness, so He would have us to be entirely His. And this is the chastity of our souls, to be consecrated and dedicated to Him. On the other hand it is a spiritual whoredom for us to turn away from Him to any superstition.

153. How is this to be understood, that He punishes the sin of the fathers on their children?

To give us a greater fear of Him. He says not only that He will inflict punishment on those who offend Him, but that their offspring also will be cursed after them.

154. But is it not contrary to the justice of God to punish someone for others?

If we consider the condition of the human race, the question is answered. For by nature we are all cursed, and we cannot complain of God when

129

He leaves us in this condition. Moreover as He manifests His grace and love toward His servants in blessing their children, so this is a testimony to His punishment of the wicked, when He leaves their seed accursed.

155. What more does He say?
To incite us by gentleness, He says that He will have mercy on all who love Him and observe His commandments, to a thousand generations.

156. Does He mean that the obedience of a faithful man will save the whole of his race, even if they are still wicked?
No, but that He will extend His goodness toward the faithful to such an extent, that in love for them He will make Himself know to their children, not only to prosper them according to the flesh, but to sanctify them by His Spirit, that He might make them obedient to His will.

157. But this is not always so.
No. For as the Lord reserves for Himself the freedom to show mercy to the children of the ungodly, so on the other hand He retains the power to elect or reject in the generation of the faithful as it seems good to Him (Rom. 9:15-22). However, He does this in such a way that men may acknowledge that this promise is not vain or fallacious (Rom. 2:6-10).

158. Why does He mention here a thousand generations, and in regard to punishment, mention only three or four?
To signify that it is His nature to exercise kindness and gentleness much more than strictness or severity, as He testifies, when He says that He is ready to show mercy, but slow to anger (Ex. 34:6-7; Ps. 103:8).

159. Let us come to the third commandment.
Thou shalt not take the name of the Lord thy God in vain.

160. What does this mean?
He forbids us to abuse the name of God, not only in perjury, but also in superfluous and idle swearing.

161. Can the name of God we used lawfully in oaths?
Yes, when they are necessary, i.e., in order to uphold the truth, when it requires it, and in maintaining love and concord among us.

162. Does He reprove no other oaths, then those which are a dishonour to God?
In this one case He gives us a general instruction never to utter the name

of God except with fear and humility in order to glorify it. For since it is holy and honourable, we ought to guard against taking the Name of God in such a way that we appear to hold it in contempt, or give others occasion to vilify it.

163. How is this to be done?
By never thinking or speaking of God and His works without honour and reverence.

164. What follows?
A warning, that He will not hold him guiltless, who takes His name in vain.

165. Since elsewhere He gives a general warning that He will punish all transgressors, what is the advantage of this warning?
He wants to declare how highly He regards the glory of His name, explicitly mentioning that He will not suffer anyone to despise it, so that we may be all the more careful to hold it in reverence.

166. Let us come to the fourth commandment.
Remember the Sabbath day, to keep it holy. Sis days shalt thou labour, and do all thy work: But the seventh is the Sabbath of the Lord thy God: in it thou shalt not do any work, thou, nor thy son, nor thy daughter, thy man-servant, nor thy maid-servant, nor thy cattle, nor thy stranger that is within thy gates: For in six days the Lord made haven and earth, the sea, and all that in them is, and rested the seventh day, and hallowed it.

167. Does He order us to labour six days a week that may rest on the seventh?
Not precisely, but in allowing us to labour for six days, He excepts the seventh, on which it is not right to be engaged in work.

168. Does He thus forbid us all work one day a week?
This commandment has a particular reason, for the observance of rest is part of the ceremonies of the ancient Law, which was abolished at the coming of Jesus Christ.

169. Do you mean that this commandment properly belongs to the Jews, and that it was given for the time of the Old Testament?
I do, in so far as it is ceremonial.

170. How is that? Is there anything else in it besides the ceremony?
It was given for three reasons.

171. What are they?
To represent spiritual rest, in aid of ecclesiastical polity, and for the relief of servants.

172. What is this spiritual rest?
It is to cease from our own works, that the Lord may work in us.

173. How is that done?
By mortifying our flesh, that is, renouncing our own nature, so that God may govern us by His Spirit.

174. Is this to be done only one day a week?
This is to be done continually. After we have once begun, we must continue all our life.

175. Why, then, is a certain day appointed to represent this?
It is not required that the representation should be altogether identical with the truth, but it is sufficient that there should be some resemblance.

176. But why is the seventh day appointed rather than any other day?
The number seven implies perfection in Scripture. Thus it is suited to denote perpetuity. It reminds us also that our spiritual rest is only begun in this life, and will not be perfect until we depart from this world.

177. But what is meant when our Lord asserts that we must rest as He did?
After having created all His works in six days, He dedicated the seventh to the contemplation of His works. And in order better to induce us to do this, He set before us His own example. For nothing is so desirable as to be conformed to Him.

178. Must we meditate continually on the works of God, or is it sufficient on one day out of seven?
We must do it every hour, but because of our weakness, one day is specially appointed. And this is the polity of which I spoke.

179. What order, then, is to be observed on that day?
That the people meet to hear the doctrine of God, to engage in common

prayer, and bear witness to their faith and religion.

180. What do you mean by saying that this commandment is also given to provide for the relief of servants?
To give some relaxation to those who are under the power of others. And likewise, this tends to maintain a common polity. For everyone accustoms himself to labour for the rest of the time, when there is one day for rest.

181. Let us now see how this commandment addresses itself to us.
As for the ceremony, it was abolished, for we have the accomplishment of it in Christ Jesus.

182. How?
Our old man is crucified, through the power of His death, and through His resurrection we are raised up to newness of life (Rom.6:6).

183. What else is there here for us?
That we observe the order constituted in the Church, to hear the Word of God, to engage in public prayers and in the Sacraments, and that we do not contravene the spiritual order among the faithful.

184. And does the figure give us any further benefit?
Yes, indeed. It should lead us to the truth, namely, that being true members of Christ, we should cease from our own works, and put ourselves under His government.

185. Let us come to the second table.
It begins, "Honour thy father and thy mother."

186. What do you mean by "honour"?
That children be humble and obedient toward their parents, doing them honour and reverence, helping them and being at their command, as they are bound.

187. Proceed further.
God adds a promise to the commandment, "That thy days may be prolonged on the land which the Lord thy God will give thee."

188. What does that mean?
That God will give long life to those who honour their father and mother

as they ought.

189. Seeing this life is full of misery, why does God promise man as a favour that he will live long?

However miserable it may be, life on earth is a blessing from God to the faithful, if only for this reason, that in it God testifies to His fatherly love in supporting them in it.

190. Does it follow conversely, that the man who dies prematurely is cursed of God?

By no means. Rather does it sometimes happen that the Lord withdraws from this world more quickly those whom He loves most.

191. In so doing, how does He fulfill His promise?

All that God promises us in earthly blessings, we must receive under this condition, viz. that it is expedient for our spiritual salvation. For it would be poor indeed if that did not precedence.

192. What of those who are rebellious against their father and mother?

Not only will God punish them at the last judgment, but here also God will exercise judgment on their bodies, it may be by letting them die before their time, or ignominiously, or in some other way.

193. Does He not speak expressly of the land of Canaan in this promise?

Yes, so far as the children of Israel are concerned, but the term ought to have a more general meaning for us. For seeing that the earth is the Lord's, whatever be the country we inhabit, He assigns it to us for our habitation (Ps. 24:1; 89:12; 115:16).

194. Is that all there is to the commandment?

Though father and mother only are mentioned, nevertheless all superiors are intended, as the reason is the same.

195. What is the reason?

That God has given them pre-eminence; for there is no authority whether of parents, or princes, or of any others who are over us, but what God has ordained (Rom. 13:1).

196. Repeat the sixth commandment.

Thou shalt not kill.

197. Does it forbid nothing but murder?

Yes, indeed. For seeing it is God who speaks, He gives us law not only for outward deeds, but primarily for the affections of our heart.

198. You mean then that there is some kind of inward murder which God forbids to us?

I do: hatred and rancour, and desire to do evil to our neighbor.

199. Is it sufficient for us not to hate or to bear ill will?

No, for in condemning hatred God signifies that He requires us to love our neighbours and seek their salvation, and all this with true affection and without simulation.

200. State the seventh commandment.

Thou shalt not commit adultery.

201. What is the essence of this?

That all fornication is cursed by God, and therefore we must abstain from it if we do not want to provoke His anger against us.

202. Does it not require anything else?

We must always regard the nature of the Lawgiver, who does not halt at the outward act, but requires the affection of the heart.

203. What more then does it mean?

Since our bodies and our souls are temples of the Holy Spirit (1 Cor. 3:16, 6:15; 2 Cor. 6:16), we must preserve them in uprightness. And so we must be chaste not only in deed, but also in desire, word and gesture. Accordingly no part of us is to be polluted with unchastity.

204. Let us come to the eighth commandment.

Thou shalt not steal.

205. Is it only meant to prohibit the thefts which are punished by justice, or does it extend further?

It refers to all civil traffic and unscrupulous means of acquiring our neighbour's good, whether by violence, or fraud, or in any other kind of way that God has not allowed.

206. Is it enough to abstain from evil deeds, or is covetousness also included here?
We must ever return to this, that the Lawgiver is spiritual, that He does not speak simply of outward thefts, but all schemes, wishes and plans to enrich ourselves at the expense of our neighbour.

207. What are to do then?
We must do our duty in preserving for every man his own.

208. What is the ninth commandment?
Thou shalt not bear false witness against thy neighbour.

209. Does it forbid perjury in court, or any kind of lying against our neighbour?
In mentioning this one case it gives a general instruction, that we are not to speak evil of our neighbour falsely, nor by our slanders and lies are we do him harm in his possessions, or in his reputations.

210. But why does He expressly mention public perjury?
That He may give us a greater abhorrence of this vice of evil speaking and slander, telling us that if a man accustom himself to slandering and defaming his neighbour, he will soon descend to perjury in court.

211. Does He only forbid evil speaking, or does He also include evil thinking?
Both of them, for the reason already stated. For whatever it is wrong to do before men, it is wrong to wish before God.

212. The summarize its meaning.
He enjoins us not to be inclined to misjudge and defame our neighbours, but rather to esteem them highly, as far as the truth will permit, and to preserve their good reputation in our speech.

213. Let us come to the last commandment.
Thou shalt not covet thy neighbour's house, thou shalt not covet thy neighbour's wife, nor his man-servant, nor his maid-servant, nor his ox, nor his ass, nor any thing that is thy neighbour's.

214. Seeing that the whole law is spiritual, as you have so often said before, and the other commandments are not only to order outward acts, but also the affections of the heart, what more is added here?
The Lord wished by the other commandments to rule our affections and

will, but here He imposes a law also on our thoughts which though charged with covetousness and desire, yet stop short of an active intention.

215. Do you mean that the least temptation that enters into the thought of a believer is sin, even though he resists it and does not consent to it?
It is certain that all evil thoughts proceed from the infirmity of our flesh, even though we do not consent to them. But I say that this commandment speaks of concupiscence which tickles and pierces the heart of man, without bringing him to a deliberate purpose.

216. You say then that the evil affections which involve a definite act of will or resolution are already condemned, but now the Lord requires of us such integrity, that no wicked desire may enter our hearts, to solicit and incite them to evil.
That is right.

217. Can we now give a short summary of the whole law?
We can, reducing it to two articles—the first of which is that we are to love God with all our heart, and with all our soul, and with all our strength; the second that we love our neighbours as ourselves.

218. What is meant by the love of God?
To love Him as God is to have and hold Him as Lord, Saviour and Father, and this requires reverence, honour, faith, and obedience along with love.

219. What does "with all our heart" signify, and "with all our soul, and with all our strength?
Such a zeal and such a vehemence, that there is in us no desire, no will, no intention and no thought, contrary to this love.

220. What is the meaning of the second article?
As we are by nature prone to love ourselves, that this affection overcomes all others, so love to our neighbour should be so predominant in our hearts, as to direct and govern us, and be the rule of all our thoughts and actions.

221. What do you understand by "our neighbours"?
Not only our parents and friends, or those acquainted with us, but also

those who are unknown to us, and even our enemies.

222. But what connection do they have with us?
That which God has placed among all men on earth, and is so inviolable, that it cannot be abolished by the malice of any man.

223. You say, then, that if any man hate us, the blame is his own, and yet according to the order of God, he does not cease to be our neighbour, and we are to regard him as such?
It is so.

224. Seeing that the law of God comprises the form of worshiping Him aright, should not the Christian man live according to its command?
Yes indeed. But there is some infirmity in us, so that no man acquits himself perfectly in it.

225. Why then does the Lord require a perfection which is beyond our ability?
He requires nothing which we are not bound to perform. Nevertheless, provided we take care to conform our life to what we are told here, although we are very far from reaching perfection, the Lord does not impute our faults to us.

226. Do you speak of all men in general, or of believers only?
He who is not yet regenerated by the Spirit of God cannot begin to do the least of the commandments. Moreover, even if a person could be found who had fulfilled some part of the law, he would not acquit himself before God, for our Lord pronounces that all those who have not fulfilled all the things contained in it, will be accursed (Deut. 27:26; Gal. 3:10).

227. Hence we must conclude that the law has a two-fold office, in accordance with the fact that there are two classes of men.
Yes, in regard to unbelievers it seems but to convict and make them inexcusable before God (Rom. 3:3). And this is what Paul says, that it is the ministry of death, and condemnation (2 Cor. 3:6,9). In regard to believers, it has a very different use.

228. What?
First, in that it shows them that they cannot justify themselves by their works, it humbles them and disposes them to seek their salvation in Jesus Christ (Rom. 3:3). Secondly, inasmuch as it requires of them much more

than they are able to perform, it admonishes them to pray unto the Lord, that He may give them strength and power (Gal. 4:6), and at the same time reminds them of their perpetual quilt, that they may not presume to be proud. Thirdly it is a kind of bridle, by which they are kept in the fear of God.

229. We say then that although during this mortal life we will never fulfill the Law, such perfection is not required of us in vain, for it shows us the mark at which we ought to aim, that each of us, according to the grace God has bestowed on him, may strive continually to press toward it, and to advance day by day.
That is as I understand it.

230. Do we not have perfect rule of goodness in the Law?
Yes, and therefore God demands nothing from us, but to follow it; and, on the other hand, repudiates and rejects all that a man undertakes to do beyond what it contains. The only sacrifice He requires is obedience (1 Sam. 15:22; Jer. 7:21-23).

231. What is the purpose then of all the admonitions, reproofs, commandments, and exhortations made both by Prophets and Apostles?
They are nothing else than declarations of the Law, leading us into obedience to it rather than turning us away from it.

232. But nothing is said about particular vocations?
When it is said that we are to render to every one his due, we may well infer what the duty of each is in his own vocation. Moreover as we have already said, this is expounded for us in the whole of Scripture, for what the Lord has set down in this summary, He treats of there, and with much fuller teaching.

III. OF PRAYER

233. Since we have spoken sufficiently of the service of God, which is the second part of His worship, let us now speak of the third part.
We said it was the invocation of God in all our needs.

234. Do you think that He alone is to be invoked?
Yes, for He requires this as the worship proper to His Deity.

235. If it is so, in what way is it legitimate for us to ask the aid of men?

There is a great difference between these two things. For we call upon God to protest that we expect no good but from Him, and that we have no refuge elsewhere, and yet we ask the assistance of men, as far as He permits, and has given them the power and means of helping us.

236. You mean that when we seek the succour of men, there is nothing to prevent our calling upon God alone, seeing that we do not put our reliance on them, and do not seek their aid except in so far as God has ordained them to be ministers and dispensers of His blessings, in order to assist us.

That is true. And indeed, every benefit that comes to us we should take as coming from God Himself, as in truth it is He who sends it to us by their hands.

237. Nevertheless, should we not give thanks to men for the kindness which they do to us?

Certainly, if only for the reason that God honours them by communicating His blessings to us through their hands, for in this way He lays us under obligation to Him, and wishes us to be mindful of them.

238. Can we not conclude from this that it is wrong to invoke angels, and saints who have departed from this world?

Yes, indeed; for God has not assigned to saints this office of aiding and assisting us. And in regard to angels, though He employs their ministry for our salvation, nevertheless He does not wish us to invoke them, nor to address ourselves to them.

239. You say, then, that all that conflicts with the order instituted by the Lord, contravenes His will?

Yes, for it is a sure sign of infidelity if we are not contented with what the Lord gives to us. Moreover, if instead of having a refuge in God alone, in obedience to His command, we have recourse to them, putting something of our reliance on them, we fall into idolatry, seeing we transfer to them that which God has reserved for Himself.

240. Let us now speak of the way of prayer to God. Is it sufficient to pray with the tongue, or does prayer require also the spirit and the heart?

The tongue is not always necessary, but there must be understanding and affection.

241. How will you prove that?
Since God is Spirit, He always requires the heart, and especially in prayer, in which we enter into communication with Him, wherefore He promises to be near to those only who call upon Him in truth (Ps. 145:18). On the other hand, He curses all who pray to Him in hypocrisy, and without affection (Isa. 29:13, 14).

242. All prayers, then, made only with the mouth are vain?
Not only vain, but also displeasing to God.

243. What kind of affection should we have in prayer?
First, that we feel our misery and poverty, and that this feeling should beget sorrow and anguish in us. Secondly, that we have an earnest desire to obtain grace from God. This desire will also kindle our hearts, and engender in us an ardent longing to pray.

244. Does this derive from our nature, or from the grace of God?
Here God must come to our aid, for we are too dull, but the Spirit of God helps us with groanings that cannot be uttered, and forms in our hearts the affection and zeal that God requires, as Paul says (Rom. 8:26; Gal. 4:6).

245. Does this mean that we have not to incite and urge ourselves to pray?
By no means. On the contrary, when we do not feel such a disposition within us we should beseech the Lord to put it into us, so as to make us capable and fit to pray as we ought.

246. You do not, however, mean that the tongue is quite useless in prayer?
Not at all, for sometimes it helps the mind, sustaining and keeping it from being drawn away from God so easily. Besides, since more than all the other members it was formed to the glory of God, it is very reasonable that it should be employed by all means for this purpose. Moreover, the zeal of the heart by its own ardour and vehemence often constrains the tongue to speak quite spontaneously.

247. If so, what about prayer in an unknown tongue?
It is a mockery of God, and a perverse hypocrisy (1 Cor. 14:14).

248. But when we pray to God, is it a venture in which we do not know whether we will succeed or not? Or ought we to be certain that our praying will be heard?

The ground of our prayers should always be, that they will received by God, and that we shall obtain what we request as far is it is expedient for us. And therefore St. Paul says that true prayer comes from faith (Rom. 10:14). For if we have no reliance upon the goodness of God, it will be impossible for us to call upon Him in truth.

249. And what of those who doubt, not knowing if God hears or not?

Their prayers are utterly void, since they have no promise, for He says that whatever we ask, believing, we shall receive (Matt. 21:22; Mark 11:24).

250. It remains to learn how and in whose name we can have the boldness to present ourselves before God, seeing that we are so unworthy in ourselves.

First we have promises on which we must rest, without considering our worthiness (Ps. 50:15; 91:3; 145:18; Isa. 30:15; 65:24; Jer. 29:12; Joel 3:5). Secondly, if we are children of God, He induces and urges us by His Holy Spirit to betake ourselves to Him familiarly, as to our Father (Matt. 9:2, 22; etc.). And lest we, who are poor worms of the earth, and miserable sinners, should be afraid to appear before His glorious majesty, He gives us our Lord Jesus Christ as a Mediator (I Tim. 2:5; Heb. 4:16; I John 2:1), that through Him we may have access and have no doubt of finding grace.

251. Do you understand that we are to call upon God only, in the Name of Jesus Christ?

I understand so, for we have an express commandment about this. And in it we are promised that by His intercession our requests will be heard (John 14:13).

252. It is not, then, temerity or foolish presumption on our part, if we presume to address God personally, seeing that we have Jesus Christ for our Advocate, and if we set Him before us, that God may for His sake be gracious to us and accept us?

No, for we pray as it were by His mouth, since He gives us entrance and audience, and intercedes for us (Rom. 8:34).

253. Let us now speak of the substance of our prayers. Can we ask for all that comes into our mind, or is there a certain rule to be

observed about it?

If we followed our fantasy, our prayers would be very badly ordered. We are so ignorant that we cannot judge what it is good to ask: Moreover, all our desires are so intemperate that it is necessary that we should not give them a loose rein.

254. What is to be done, then?

That God Himself should instruct us, according to what He knows to be expedient; that we do nothing but follow Him, as if He were leading us by the hand.

255. What instructions has He given?

He has given us ample instructions throughout Scripture; but that we may address ourselves the better to a definite end, He has given us a form in which He has briefly comprehended everything that is legitimate and expedient for us to pray for.

256. Repeat it.

Our Lord Jesus Christ, being asked by His Disciples to teach them how to pray, answered that they should pray thus (Matt. 6:9-13; Luke 11:1-4): "Our Father, which art in heaven, hallowed by thy name. Thy kingdom come. Thy will be done, as it is in heaven. Give us this day our daily bread. And forgive us our debts, as we forgive our debtors. And lead us not into temptation; but deliver us from evil: For thine is the kingdom, and the power, and the glory, for ever. Amen."

257. To make it easier to understand, tell me how many sentences it contains.

Six, of which the first three concern the glory of God alone, without any reference to ourselves; the other three are for us, and concern our blessing and profit.

258. Are we then to ask God for anything from which no benefit redounds to us?

It is true that God, by His infinite goodness, so arranges and orders things, that nothing tends to the glory of His Name without being also salutary to us. Therefore, when His name is sanctified, He turns it to our sanctification; when His Kingdom comes, we are, in a way, sharers in it. But in desiring and asking all these things, we ought to have regard only for His glory, without thinking of ourselves, or seeking our own profit.

259. According to what you say, the first three of these requests are expedient for us, and yet they ought not to be made with any other intention that of desiring that God may be glorified.

It is so. And similarly, although the last three requests are appointed as prayers for what is expedient to us, yet even in them we ought to seek the glory of God, so that it may be the end of all our desires.

260. Let us come to the exposition. And before we go any further, why is God called our Father, rather than by some other name?

Since it is essential that our consciences have a steadfast assurance, when we pray, our God gives Himself a name. which suggests only gentleness and kindness, in order to take away from us all doubt and anxiety, and to give us boldness in coming to Him personally.

261. Shall we then dare to go to God familiarly, as a child to his father?

Yes, in fact with greater assurance of obtaining what we ask. For if we, being evil, cannot refuse our children bread and meat, when they ask, how much less will our heavenly Father, who is not only good, but sovereign goodness itself (Matt. 7:11).

262. Can we not prove from this very Name, what has been said, viz. that prayer should be grounded on the intercession of Jesus Christ?

Yes, certainly. For God does not acknowledge us as His children, except in so far as we are members of His Son.

263. Why do you not call God your God, but call Him our Father together?

Each believer may indeed call Him his own Father, but in this formula Jesus Christ instructs us to pray together, to remind us that in our prayers we are to exercise charity towards our neighbours, and not only to care for ourselves.

264. What is meant by the clause "who art in heaven"?

It is just the same as if I were to call Him exalted, mighty, incomprehensible.

265. To what end, and for what reason?

That when we call upon Him, we may learn to lift our thoughts on high, and not to have any carnal or earthly thoughts of Him, not to measure Him by our apprehension, nor to subject Him to our will, but to adore His glorious Majesty in humility. It teaches us also to have more reliance on Him, since He is Governor and Master of all.

266. Now expound the first petition.
The Name of God is His renown, with which He is celebrated among men. We pray then that His glory may be exalted above all, and in all things.

267. Do you think that His glory can increase or decrease?
Not in itself. But this means that it may be manifested, as it ought to be, that all the works which God performs may appear glorious, as indeed they are, so that He Himself may be glorified in every way.

268. What do you understand by the Kingdom of God in the second petition?
It consists principally of two things: that He leads His own, and governs them by His Spirit, and on the other hand casts down and confounds the reprobate who refuse to subject themselves to His rule, and so makes it clear that there is no power which can resist His power.

269. In what sense do you pray that this Kingdom may come?
That day by day the Lord may increase the numbers of the faithful, that day by day He may increasingly bestow His graces upon them, until He has filled them completely; moreover, that He cause His truth to shine more and more and manifest His justice, so that Satan and the powers of darkness may be put to confusion, and all iniquity be destroyed and abolished.

270. Is that not taking place today?
Yes indeed—in part, but we pray that it may continually increase and advance, until at last it comes to its perfection in the day of judgment, in which God alone will be exalted, and ever creature will be humbled before His Majesty, and He will be all in all (I Cor. 15:28).

271. What do you mean by asking that the will of God may be done?
That all creatures may be brought under obedience to Him, and so that everything may be done according to His good will.

272. Do you mean that nothing can be done contrary to His will?
We ask not only that He may bring all things to pass, as He has determined in His counsel, but also that, putting down all rebellion, He may bring all wills to conform to His own.

273. In so doing, do we not renounce our own wills?

We do, not only that He may overthrow our desires, which are at variance with His own good will, bringing them all to nought, but also that He may create in us new spirits and new hearts, so that we may will nothing of ourselves, but rather that His Spirit may will in us, and bring us into full agreement with Him.

274. Why do you add "on earth as it is in heaven"?

Since His heavenly creatures or His angels have it as their own object to obey Him, promptly without opposition, we desire that the same thing may be done on earth, that is, that all men may yield themselves in voluntary obedience.

275. Let us come to the second part. What mean you by "the daily bread" you ask for?

In general, everything that we need for our body, not only food and clothing, but all that God knows to be expedient for us, that we may be able to eat our bread in peace.

276. But why do you ask God to give you your food, when He orders us to win it, by working with our hands?

Though He commands us to work for our living, nevertheless it is not our labour, industry, and diligence, that provide us with food, but the blessing of God alone, which makes the labour of our hands to prosper. Moreover we ought to understand that it is not meat that nourishes us, although we have it owing to His command, but the power of the Lord alone who uses it as His instrument (Deut. 8:3, 17).

277. Why do you call it yours, when you ask God to give it to you?

Because of the kindness of God it becomes ours, though it is by no means due to us. We are also reminded by this not to desire the bread of others, but only that which we acquire by legitimate means, according to the ordinance of God.

278. Why do you say "daily" and "this day"?

That we may learn to be content, and not to covet more than our need requires.

279. Since this prayer is common to all, how can the rich, who have an abundance of good things, provide for a long time, ask for bread each day?

The rich, as well as the poor, should understand that none of the things profit them, unless the Lord grant them the use of them, and by His grace make it profitable to them. Thus in having we have nothing, unless He gives it to us.

280. What does the fifth petition contain?
That it pleases God to pardon our sins.

281. Is any man living so righteous, that He does not need to make this petition?
No, for the Lord Jesus gave this form of prayer to His Apostles for His Church. Wherefore he who would exempt himself from this, must renounce the community of Christians. And indeed Scripture testifies to us that even the most perfect man seeking to justify himself before God in a single matter, will be found guilty in a thousand (Job 9:3). Thus the only refuge we may have is in His mercy.

282. How do you think that such remission is granted to us?
As the words of Jesus Christ used declare: because our sins are debts, making us liable to eternal death, we pray that God will pardon us out of His sheer kindness.

283. You mean, them, that it is by the gratuitous goodness of God that we obtain remission of sins?
Yes, for we can offer no satisfaction for the smallest sin we commit, if God does no exercise His sheer kindness toward us in forgiving us them all.

284. What gain and profit do we receive, when God pardons our sins?
We are acceptable to Him, just as if we were righteous and innocent, and our consciences are assured of His paternal love, from which comes salvation and life.

285. When you pray that He may forgive us as we forgive our debtors, do you mean that in pardoning men we merit pardon from God?
By no means, for then pardon would not be by grace, and would not be founded, as it ought to be, on the satisfaction which Jesus Christ made for us in His death. But since by forgetting the injuries done to ourselves, we follow His gentleness and clemency, and so demonstrate that we are His children, God has given us this as a sign in confirmation that we are His children. On the other hand, He indicates to us that we cannot expect

anything at His judgment but utter severity and extreme rigour, if we are not ready to pardon and show mercy to others who are guilty toward us.

286. Do you think, then, God refuses to have as His children those who cannot forget the offenses committed against them, so that they cannot hope to be partakers of His grace?
Yes. And He intends that all men may know that with what measure they mete to their neighbours, it shall be measured to them.

287. What follows?
"Lead us not into temptation, but deliver us from evil."

288. Do you treat this as one petition?
Yes, for the second part is an explanation of the first part.

289. What is the substance of it?
That God does not allow us to fall to evil, or permit us to be overcome by the Devil, and the lustful desires of our flesh, which strive against us (Rom. 7:23), but He gives us strength to resist, sustains us by His hand, takes us into His safe keeping, to defend and lead us.

290. How is this done?
When He governs us by His Spirit, to make us love the good, and hate the evil, follow justice, and flee from sin. By the power of His Spirit, we may overcome the Devil, sin and the flesh.

291. Do we stand in need of this?
Yes, for the Devil continually watches for us, like a roaring lion ready to devour us (I Peter 5:8). We are so feeble and frail that he would immediately overcome us, if God did not fortify us, that we might be victorious over him.

292. What does the word "temptation" signify?
The wiles and assaults of the Devil, which he uses to attack us, seeing that our natural judgment is prone to be deceived and to deceive us, and our will is always ready to addict itself to evil rather than to good.

293. But why do you pray God not to lead you into evil, when this is the proper office of Satan the Devil?
As God by His mercy preserves the faithful, and does not permit the devil to seduce them, or sin to overcome them, so those whom He means to punish He not only abandons, and deprives of His grace, but also

yields to the Devil to be subjected to his tyranny, blinds them and delivers them over to a reprobate mind.

294. What is intended by the addition, "For thine is the kingdom, and the power, and the glory, for ever"?

To remind us again that our prayers are altogether grounded on the power and goodness of God, and not on ourselves, for we are not worthy to open our mouth in prayer; and also that we may learn to close our prayers in His praise.

295. Is it lawful to ask anything else, not mentioned here?

Although we are free to use other words, and another form and manner, yet not prayer will ever please God which does not correspond to this as the only rule of right prayer.

IV. THE WORD OF GOD

296. It is time to come to the fourth part of worship we are to render to God.

We said that this consists in acknowledging with the heart and confirming with the mouth that God is the author of all good, that thereby we may glorify Him.

297. Has He given us any rule for this?

All the praises and thanksgivings contained in Scripture ought to be our rule and guide.

298. Is there nothing regarding this in the Lord's Prayer?

Yes there is, for when we pray that His name may be hallowed, we pray that He may be glorified in all His works, as indeed He is–that He may be praised for His justice when He punishes, for His mercy when He pardons, and for His faithfulness when He fulfils His promises; in short, that there is nothing in which His glory does not shine forth. This is to ascribe to Him the praise for all blessing.

299. What shall we infer from all that we have said?

What truth itself tells us, and was stated at the outset, viz. that this is eternal life to know one true God the Father, and Jesus Christ whom He has sent (John 17:3)—to know Him, I say, in order that we may worship Him aright, that He may be not only our Master, but also our Father and Saviour, and we be in turn His children and servants, and a people dedicated to His glory.

300. How can we attain to such a blessedness?
For this end God has left us His holy Word, which is, as it wee, an entry into His heavenly Kingdom.

301. Where do you find this Word?
It is comprised for us in the Holy Scriptures.

302. How are we to use it in order to profit by it?
By receiving it with the full consent of our conscience, as truth come down from heaven, submitting ourselves to it in right obedience, loving it with a true affection by having it imprinted in our hearts, we may follow it entirely and conform ourselves to it.

303. Is all this within our own power?
None of it; but God works them in us in this way by His Holy Spirit.

304. But are we not to take trouble and be diligent, and zealously strive by hearing and reading its teaching, as it is declared to us?
Yes, indeed: first each one of us in particular ought to study it: and above all, we are frequently to attend the sermons in which this Word is expounded in the Assembly of the Christians.

305. Do you mean that it is not enough for people to read it privately at home, without altogether hearing its teaching in common?
That is just what I mean, while God provides the way for it.

306. Why do you say that?
Because Jesus Christ has established this order in His Church (Eph. 4:11), and He has declared this to be the only means of edifying and preserving it. Thus we must keep ourselves to it and not be wiser than our Master.

307. Is it necessary, then, that there should be pastors?
Yes; and that we should hear them, receiving the teaching of the Lord in humility by their mouth. Therefore whoever despises them and refuses to hear them, rejects Jesus Christ, and separates himself from the fellowship of the faithful (Matt. 10:40; Luke 10:16).

308. But is it enough to have been instructed by them once, or ought he to continue to do this?

It is little to have begun, unless you go on to persevere. We must continue to be disciples of Christ right to the end. But He has ordained the ministers of the Church to teach in His Name.

V. OF THE SACREMENTS

309. Is there no other means than the Word by which God communicates Himself to us?

To the preaching of His Word He has conjoined the Sacraments.

310. What is a Sacrament?

An outward attestation of the grace of God which, by a visible sign, represents spiritual things to imprint the promises of God more firmly in our hearts, and to make us more sure of them.

311. What? Does a visible and natural sign have this power to assure the conscience?

No, not of itself, but in so far as it is ordained of God for this end.

312. Seeing it is the proper office of the Holy Spirit to seal the promises of God in our hearts, how do you attribute this to the Sacraments?

There is a great difference between the one and the other. The Spirit of God in very truth is the only One who can touch and move our hearts, enlighten our minds, and assure our consciences; so that all this ought to be judged as His own work, that praise may be ascribed to Him alone. Nevertheless, the Lord Himself makes use of the Sacraments as inferior instruments according as it seems good to Him, without in any way detracting from the power of the Holy Spirit.

313. You think, then, that the efficacy of the Sacraments does not consist in the outward element, but proceeds entirely from the Spirit of God?

Yes; for the Lord is pleased to work by these instruments which He has instituted: without detracting from His own power.

314. And what moves God to do that?

For the alleviation of our weaknesses. If we were spiritual by nature, like the angels, we could behold God and His graces. But as we are bound up with our bodies, it is needful for us that God should make use of figures to represent to us spiritual and heavenly things, for otherwise we could not comprehend them. At the same time, it is expedient for us to have all our senses exercised in His Holy promises, in order to confirm us in them.

315. Since God has introduced the Sacraments to meet our need, it would be arrogance and presumption to think that we could dispense with them.
Certainly: hence he who voluntarily abstains from using them thinks that he has no need of them, condemns Jesus Christ, rejects His grace, and quenches His Holy Spirit.

316. But what assurance of grace can the Sacraments give, seeing that good and bad both receive them?
Although the unbelievers and the wicked make of none effect the grace offered them through the Sacraments, yet it does not follow that the proper nature of the Sacraments is also made of non effect.

317. How, then, and when do the Sacraments produce this effect?
When we receive them in faith, seeking Jesus Christ alone and His grace in them.

318. Why do you say that we must seek Jesus Christ in them?
I mean that we are not to be taken up with the earthly sign so as to seek our salvation in it, nor are we to imagine that it has a peculiar power enclosed within it. On the contrary, we are to employ the sign as a help, to lead us directly to the Lord Jesus, that we may find in Him our salvation and all our well-being.

319. Seeing that faith is required, why do you say that they are given to confirm us in faith, to assure us of the promises of God?
It is not sufficient for faith once to be generated in us. It must be nourished and sustained, that it may grow day by day and be increased within us. To nourish, strengthen, and increase it, God gives us the Sacraments. This is what Paul indicates when he says that they are used to seal the promises of God in our hearts (Rom. 4:11).

320. But is it not a sign of unbelief when the promises of God are not firm enough for us, without support?
It is a sign of the smallness and weakness of faith, and such is indeed the faith of the children of God, who do not, however, cease to be faithful, although their faith is still imperfect. As long as we live in this world some elements of unfaithfulness remain in our flesh, and therefore we

must always advance and grow in faith.

321. How many Sacraments are there in the Christian Church?
There are only two Sacraments common to all which the Lord Jesus has instituted for the whole company of the faithful.

322. What are they?
Baptism and the Holy Supper.

323. What likeness and difference is there between them?
Baptism is for us a kind of entrance into the Church of God, for it testifies that instead of our being strangers to Him, God receives us as members of His family. The Supper testifies that God as a good Father carefully feeds and refreshes the members of His household.

324. That the meaning may be more clear to us, let us treat of them separately. First, what is the meaning of Baptism?
It consists of two parts. The Lord represents to us in it, first, the forgiveness of our sins (Eph. 5:26, 27) and, secondly, our regeneration or spiritual renewal (Rom. 6:4).

325. What resemblance has water with these things in order to represent them?
The forgiveness of sins is a kind of washing, by which our souls are cleansed from their defilements, just as the stains of the body are washed away by water.

326. What about the other part?
The beginning of our regeneration and its end is our becoming new creatures, through the Spirit of God. Therefore the water is poured on the head as a sign of death, but in such a way that our resurrection is also represented, for instead of being drowned in water, what happens to us is only for a moment.

327. You do not mean that the water is a washing of the soul.
By no means, for that pertains to the blood of Christ alone, which was shed in order to wipe away all our stains and render us pure and unpolluted before God (I John 1:7; I Peter 1:19). This is fulfilled in us when our consciences are sprinkled by the Holy Spirit. But by the Sacrament that is sealed to us.

328. Do you think that the water is only a figure to us?

It is such a figure that the reality is conjoined with it, for God does not promise us anything in vain. Accordingly it is certain that in Baptism the forgiveness of sins is offered to us and we receive it.

329. Is this grace fulfilled indiscriminately in all?

No, for some make it of no effect by their perversity. Nevertheless, the Sacrament loses nothing of its nature, although none but believers feel its efficacy.

330. From what does regeneration get its power?

From the death and resurrection of Christ. His death has had this effect, that through it our old Adam is crucified, and our evil nature is, as it were, buried, so that it no longer has the strength to rule over us. And the renewal of our life, in obedience to the righteousness of God, derives from the resurrection of Christ.

331. How is this grace applied to us in Baptism?

In it we are clothed with Jesus Christ, and receive His Spirit, provided that we do not make ourselves unworthy of the promises given to us in it.

332. What is the proper use of Baptism on our part?

It consists in faith and in repentance. That is, assurance that we have our spiritual purity in Christ, and in feeling within us, and declaring to our neighbours by our works, that His Spirit dwells in us to mortify our natural desires and bring us to follow the Will of God.

333. If this is required, how is it that we baptize infants?

It is not said that faith and repentance should always precede the reception of the Sacrament, but they are only required from those who are capable of them. It is sufficient, then, if infants produce and manifest the fruit of their Baptism after they come to the age of discretion.

334. Can you show that there is nothing inconsistent in this?

Circumcision was also a Sacrament of repentance, as Moses and the prophets declare (Deut. 10:16; 30:6; Jer. 4:4); and was a Sacrament of faith, as St. Paul says (Rom. 4:11, 12). And yet God has not excluded little children from it.

335. But can you show that they are now admitted to Baptism for the same reason as in the case of circumcision?

Yes, for the promises which God anciently gave to His people of Israel are now extended to the whole world.

336. But does it follow from this that we are to use the sign also?
That becomes evident when everything is considered. Jesus Christ has not made us partakers of His grace, which formerly had been bestowed on the people of Israel, in order to diminish it in us, or make it more obscure, but rather to manifest it and to bestow it upon us in increased abundance.

337. Do you reckon that if we denied Baptism to little infants, the grace of God would then be diminished by the coming of Christ?
Yes; for the sign of the bounty and mercy of God toward our children, which they had in ancient times, would be wanting in our case, the very sign which ministers so greatly to our consolation, and to confirm the promise already given in the Command.

338. You mean then that since God in ancient times declared Himself to be the Saviour of little infants, and wanted to have this promise sealed on their bodies by an external Sacrament, it is right that confirmation of it should not be less after the advent of Christ, since the same promise remains and indeed is more clearly attested by the Word and ratified in action.
Yes. And besides, since it is quite evident that the power and the substance of Baptism pertain to little children, to deny them the sign, which is inferior to the substance, would be to do them injury.

339. On what conditions should we baptize little children?
As a sign and testimony that they are heirs of God's blessing promised to the seed of the faithful, that when they come of age they are to acknowledge the truth of their Baptism, in order to derive benefit from it.

340. Let us speak of the Supper. And, first, what is its signification?
Our Lord instituted it to assure us that by the communication of His body and blood, our souls are nourished, in the hope of eternal life.

341. But why does the Lord represent His body by the bread and His blood by the wine?
To signify that as it is the particular virtue of bread to nourish our bodies, to refresh and sustain us in this mortal life, so it pertains to His body to act toward our souls, i.e., in nourishing and quickening them spiritually, so His blood is our joy, our refreshing and our spiritual strength.

342. Do you mean that we must truly communicate in the body and blood of the Lord?

I understand so. But since the whole affiance of our salvation rests in the obedience which He has rendered to God, His Father, in order that it may be imputed to us as if it were ours, we must possess Him: for His blessings are not ours, unless He gives Himself to us first.

343. But did He not give Himself to us when He exposed Himself to death, to reconcile us to God His Father, and deliver us from damnation?

That is true; but it is not enough for us unless we receive Him, in order that we may feel in ourselves the fruit and the efficacy of His death and passion.

344. Is not the way to receive Him by faith?

Yes. Not only in believing that He died and rose again, in order to deliver us from eternal death, and acquire life for us, but also that He dwells in us, and conjoined with us in a union as the Head with the members, that by virtue of this conjunction He may make us partakers of all His grace.

345. Does this communion take place apart from the Supper alone?

Yes, indeed, we have it through the Gospel, as St. Paul declares (I Cor. 1:9): in that the Lord Jesus Christ promises us in it, that we are flesh of His flesh and bone of His bone (Eph. 5:30), that He is that living bread which came down from heaven to nourish our souls (John 6:51), and that we are one with Him, as He is one with the Father (John 17:21).

346. What is the blessing that we have in the Sacrament, and what more does it minister to us?

This communion is more abundantly confirmed in us, ratified as it were, for although Jesus Christ is truly communicated to us both by Baptism and by the Gospel, nevertheless this only in part, and not fully.

347. What then fully do we have through the sign of the bread?

That the body of the Lord Jesus which was once offered to reconcile us to God, is now given to us, to certify to us that we have part in this reconciliation.

348. What do we have in the sign of the wine?

That the Lord Jesus, who once shed His blood in payment and satisfaction for our offences, gives it to us to drink, that we may have no doubt at all of receiving its fruit.

349. According to your replies, the Supper takes us back to the death and passion of Jesus Christ, that we may communicate in its virtue?
Yes, for then the unique and perpetual sacrifice was offered for our redemption. Therefore there remains for us nought but to enjoy it.

350. The Supper, then, was not instituted in order to offer up the body of Jesus the Son to the Father?
No, for this office pertains to none but Him alone, since He is the eternal Priest (Heb. 5:5). But He commands us only to receive His body, not to offer it (Matt. 26:26).

351. Why is there a double sign?
Our Lord has appointed it for the sake of our weakness, in order to teach us that He is not only food to our souls, but drink also, so that we may seek our nourishment wholly and entirely in Him, and not elsewhere.

352. Should all men equally use the second sign, that is the chalice?
Yes, this is according to the commandment of Jesus Christ, against which nothing is to be attempted.

353. Do we have in the Supper simply the testimony of the things already mentioned, or are they truly given to us in it?
See that Jesus Christ is the Truth, there can be no doubt that the promises which He made at the Supper, are actually fulfilled in it, and that what He figures in it is made true. Thus in accordance with what He promises and represents in the Sacrament, I do not doubt that He makes us partakers of His very substance, in order to unite us with Himself in one life.

354. But how can this be, when the body of Jesus Christ is in heaven, and we are pilgrims on this earth?
By the incomprehensible power of His Spirit, who conjoins things separated by distance.

355. You do not think, then, either that the body is enclosed in the bread, or the blood in the chalice?
No. On the contrary, in order to have the reality of the Sacraments, we must lift up our hearts on high to heaven, where Jesus Christ is in the glory of His Father, from whence we expect Him in our redemption, and

do not seek Him in these corruptible elements.

356. You understand, then, that there are two things in this Sacrament, material bread and wine, which we see by the eye, handle by the hands, and perceive by the taste, and Jesus Christ by whom our souls are inwardly nourished?
Yes, but in such a way that we have in it also a testimony and a kind of pledge for the resurrection of our bodies, in that they are made partakers in the sign of life.

357. What is the right use of this Sacrament?
That which St. Paul declares, namely that a man examine himself before he approach to it (I Cor. 11:28).

358. In what is he to examine himself?
Whether he is a true member of Jesus Christ.

359. By what sign can he know this?
If he has a true faith and repentance, if he loves his neighbour in true charity, and is not tainted by hatred or rancour or discord.

360. But is it necessary to have perfect faith and charity?
Both should be entire and unfeigned, but to have such a perfection, from which nothing is wanting, will not be found among men. Moreover the Supper would have been instituted in vain if no one could receive it unless he were entirely perfect.

361. Imperfection, then, does not prevent us from approaching it.
On the contrary, the Supper would be of no use to us, if we were not imperfect. It is an aid and support for our weakness.

362. Do these two Sacraments not serve another end?
Yes, they do. They are also signs and marks of our profession. That is to say, by them we declare that we are of the people of God, and make confession of our Christianity.

363. How ought we to judge a man who never wishes to use it?
He could not be regarded as a Christian, for in so doing he refuses to confess himself as such, and tacitly, as it were, disavows Jesus Christ.

364. Is it sufficient to receive each once?
Baptism is only ordered to be received once, and may not lawfully be

repeated. But this is not so with the Supper.

365. What is the reason for that?
By Baptism God introduces and receives us into His Church. After He has received us, He signifies by the Supper that He wishes continually to nourish us.

366. To whom does it belong truly to baptize and administer the Supper?
To those who are publicly charged to teach in the Church. For the preaching of the Word and the distribution of the Sacraments are things conjoined.

367. Is there any certain proof for this?
Yes, indeed. Our Lord specially charged His Apostles to baptize as well as to preach (Matt. 28:19). In regard to the Supper. He ordered all to follow His example. Moreover He performed the office of a minister in order to give it to others.

368. But ought pastors, who are appointed to dispense the Sacraments, to admit without discretion all who present themselves there?
In regard to Baptism, as it is administered today only to infants, there is no need for discrimination; but in the Supper the minister ought to take heed not to give it to a man whom he recognizes to be entirely unworthy.

369. Why so?
Because it would pollute and dishonour the Sacrament.

370. But our Lord admitted Judas to the Supper, impious though he was?
His iniquity was still hidden, and although our Lord knew it, yet it was not evident to all.

371. What then is to be done with hypocrites?
The minister cannot exclude them as unworthy, but must wait until God has revealed their iniquity.

372. But what if he knows or has been warned that someone is unworthy?
That would not be sufficient to exclude him, unless there were a

legitimate investigation and decision of the Church.

373. Then there ought to be some order and polity regarding this.
Yes, if the Church is to be well ordered. Some persons must be appointed to watch out for the offences that may be committed. And they, with the authority of the Church, should refuse communion to those who are quite unfit, and to whom communion cannot be given without dishonouring God and scandalizing the faithful.

ABOUT THE AUTHOR

Sonny L. Hernandez is the director of Reforming America Ministries, which is an apologetics ministry that is dedicated to proclaiming the gospel, and defending the faith against all anti-Christian worldviews. He earned a doctorate from Tennessee Temple University and has written several books. The most important ministry in his life is to his wife and son.

Solus Christus!

"But when he came to himself, he said, '**How many of my father's hired servants have bread enough and to spare, and I perish with hunger! I will arise and go to my father, and will say to him, "Father, I have sinned against heaven and before you, and I am no longer worthy to be called your son. Make me like one of your hired servants."'** "And he arose and came to his father. **But when he was still a great way off, his father saw him and had compassion, and ran and fell on his neck and kissed him**. And the son said to him, 'Father, I have sinned against heaven and in your sight, and am no longer worthy to be called your son.' "But the father said to his servants, 'Bring out the best robe and put *it* on him, and put a ring on his hand and sandals on *his* feet. And bring the fatted calf here and kill *it,* and let us eat and be merry; for this my son was dead and is alive again; he was lost and is found.' And they began to be merry. "Now his older son was in the field. And as he came and drew near to the house, he heard music and dancing. So he called one of the servants and asked what these things meant. And he said to him, 'Your brother has come, and because he has received him safe and sound, your father has killed the fatted calf.' "But he was angry and would not go in. Therefore his father came out and pleaded with him. So he answered and said to *his* father, 'Lo, these many years I have been serving you; I never transgressed your commandment at any time; and yet you never gave me a young goat, that I might make merry with my friends. But as soon as this son of yours came, who has devoured your livelihood with harlots, you killed the fatted calf for him.' "And he said to him, '**Son, you are always with me, and all that I have is yours. It was right that we should make merry and be glad, for your brother was dead and is alive again, and was lost and is found**'" (Luke 15:17-32).

37281444R00095